# GULF STATES

KUWAIT · BAHRAIN · QATAR
UNITED ARAB EMIRATES · OMAN
SAUDI ARABIA · YEMEN

## JPMGUIDES

Out-of-the-ordinary desert sports

# CONTENTS

Hospitable people

Timeless traditions

Islamic architecture

# THIS WAY GULF STATES

The sensitive bridge of water separating the Arab States and Iran is a comparatively young sea, created around 4 million years ago. The Gulf varies in width between 55 and 340 km (34 to 212 miles), extending for nearly 990 km (615 miles) from its mouth off the Strait of Hormuz to its headwaters in the Shatt al-Arab delta in southern Iraq.

With a total population of around 38 million, the Arab States on the western Gulf coast consist of Kuwait, Bahrain, Qatar, Oman, the United Arab Emirates (UAE) and Saudi Arabia. The Republic of Yemen adds another 21 million. While Saudi Arabia does not grant individual tourist visas and has only recently introduced group visas, the other Gulf states are experiencing a visitor boom. In recent years the tourism and leisure industry has become a viable ontributor to the gross domestic product, historically based on some of the world's largest oil and gas reserves.

The climate between Kuwait, at the head of the Gulf, and Oman, bordering the Arabian Sea, varies considerably during the period from December to March. Temperatures at this time can drop to zero at night, but in the Lower Gulf most days are warm enough to enjoy water sports, while the best weather is to be found in the province of Dhofar in southern Oman. Summer, the low tourist season, is without exception very hot, with temperatures averaging 40–48°C between June and August. The dry heat inland is easier to bear than the coastal humidity, which tends to sap your strength, though everywhere—hotels, offices, shops and cars—is air-conditioned. The best all-round time to visit the Gulf falls between November and March when most days are sunny.

Visitors to the Gulf States rate the majesty of the desert landscape high on the list of the many attractions, which also include archaeological sites, world-class sports facilities—in particular in Dubai—excellent shopping opportunities and a balmy winter climate, all in a safe environment.

Of Swedish design, Kuwait's iconic towers are used for water storage, but the highest has a revolving observation deck.

istockphoto.com/Lingbeek van Kranen

# KUWAIT

Behind its improbable landmark of a trio of public-utility towers, Kuwait City is a gleaming capital of highrises, hugging the shores of the upper Arabian Peninsula. Among the modern palaces, cavernous mosques, shiny shopping malls and office buildings, you may perceive remnants of old city ramparts and walled-in residences tucked away in corners of urban development. A web of six- and eight-lane motorways fans out from the capital.

## Resolutely Modern

Bordered by Iraq, Saudi Arabia and the clear turquoise waters of the Gulf along its eastern coastline, Kuwait is a small country. Its 17,800 sq km (6,880 sq miles) are mostly desert, a sprawling, empty expanse with only a tiny settlement of black Bedouin tents here and there on a faraway horizon. Until the discovery of oil, fishing and pearl diving were the principal occupations, which strengthened the region's trading prominence long ago and put it on the map as an important transit point for merchants voyaging between Asia and Europe.

Nowadays, oil plays the major role in the Kuwaiti economy; the Burgan oil fields are the world's second largest after those of Ghawar in Saudi Arabia and account for more than half of the country's oil reserves. After the Gulf War of the 1990s, when Iraqi Occupation forces set ablaze 749 oil wells, more than 2 million barrels of black gold were pumped every day from the Burgan fields, once the massive mopping up operations had been completed. But in recent times it was revealed that production has dropped to 1.7 million barrels and it is estimated that Burgan will be exhausted in 30 to 40 years time.

The National Assembly represents the only elected parliament of all the Gulf States, while the Emir of Kuwait heads a dynasty that traces its origins to 1752. To keep the country humming, a huge foreign workforce is necessary: of the estimated 2.9 million inhabitants of the Emirate, only about a third are Kuwaiti.

# A BRIEF HISTORY

**2000 BC**
Failaka, the largest of the country's nine islands, is a trading station and possibly an outpost of the fabled Bahrain-based Dilmun civilization.

**4th century BC**
Under Alexander the Great, the Greeks settle on Failaka and give it the name Ikaros. It becomes a fishing and pearling centre.

**17th century**
Around 1672, the ruler of the Bani Khalid tribe, Barrak bin Ghurian, builds a *kut,* a small fortress, on the mainland.

**18th–19th centuries**
Several tribes migrate to the area, among them the Bani Utubi, comprised of several subgroups including the Al-Sabah, Al-Khalifa and Al-Zayed families. Ending a period of tumultuous rivalry, Sheikh Al Sabah bin Jaber is unanimously chosen around 1753 to administer justice and handle affairs of state. The Ottomans try to absorb Kuwait into their empire, without success.

Sheikh Mubarak signs an agreement with Britain in 1899, by which, in exchange for the Royal Navy's protection, he gives Britain responsibility for the country's foreign affairs.

**20th century–present**
In the 1920s, the ikhwan brotherhood, with the support of Abdul Aziz Al-Saud, attempts to incorporate Kuwait, and a defensive wall is quickly built around Kuwait City. Britain relinquishes its rights in 1961 and the country becomes independent. Oil revenues increase in the 1960s and 70s and a high standard of living is achieved.

Kuwait is attacked and overrun by Iraqi forces on August 2, 1990, obliging the ruling family to flee across the border to Saudi Arabia. A few weeks later, Iraq declares Kuwait its 19th province, prompting a US-led international coalition force to conduct six-week air and ground attacks to rout the occupier and liberate the country on 27 February, 1991. Nearly 800 oil wells are set ablaze by the retreating Iraqi army; they take 8 months to extinguish. In November 1994, Iraq accepts the frontier with Kuwait imposed by the UN.

In July 2003, the offices of crown prince and prime minister are separated. In May 2005, women win the right to vote.

# Sightseeing

## Kuwait City

In the heart of Kuwait City, the uninspiring main street, Fahd al-Salem, is bordered by cheap shops and modest glass and steel office buildings which sprouted in a hurry after the oil boom of the 1970s. Remains of one of the city's five gates from the 1920 walls sit on top of a roundabout mound at the foot of the boulevard.

The Arabian Gulf Road follows the coastline for miles around the bays before turning southwards. The large white edifice with sloping roof is the **National Assembly Building,** badly damaged during the Second Gulf War but now restored, and the meeting place of the Gulf's only elected parliament. It was designed by Jørn Utzon, of Sydney Opera House fame. Offshore you can see the ship that once served as the luxury Al-Salem Hotel, permanently moored here but completely burned out by the Iraqis in 1990–91.

The **National Museum**, once a priceless showcase of Islamic art, now stands grimly empty as a reminder of the looting and vandalism of the Gulf War. Part of the building is being restored to display whatever the government can manage to gather together. Nearby, the tumbledown **Sadu House**, a century old, contains a collection of Bedouin women's woven goods. Next door is the spacious **Al-Bader House**, built between 1838 and 1848, with fine examples of old carved wooden doors, thatched ceilings, stables, modest-sized living quarters but wide courtyards.

To get an idea of what the old settlement of Kuwait would have looked like, a **replica town** has been set up, where children like to play; it is also used for traditional cultural events. Nearby in the **dhow harbour**, scores of venerable teakwood vessels anchored together await sunset, when they head out to sea for a night of fishing. Other traditional boats are used for transport of goods between Kuwait and the Emirates, Iran and West India.

**Sief Palace** is the seat of the Emir's court, where his day-to-day business is carried out. Opposite is the truly **Grand Mosque**, built in 1986 at a cost of nearly $40 million to accommodate 10,000 worshippers.

Designed by Swedish architects, the **Kuwait Towers** on the headland are visible from every direction. The pair on the coast are intended for the city's water storage. The highest globe, at a height of 122 m (400 ft), is a revolving observation deck, offering a breathtaking panoramic view over the Gulf and environs

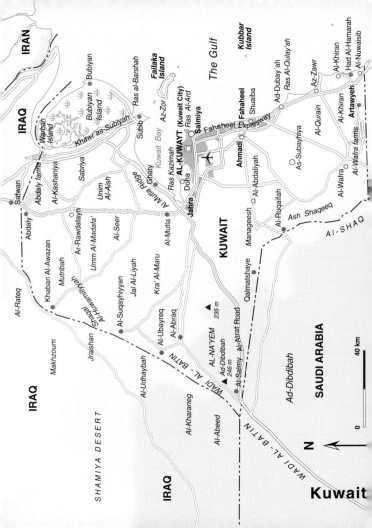

# Kuwait

of Kuwait City. The lower globe, at 88 m (289 ft), contains a restaurant. The nearby spike tower handles the city's electricity requirements and lights up the other two. But the highest peak on the skyline is the Telecommunications, or **Liberation Tower**, at 370 m (1,214 ft), in the centre of town. Its revolving viewing platform gives a lookout point almost 30 m (100 ft) higher than that of the water towers.

Beneath the Kuwait Towers is **Aqua Park**, providing hours of fun and entertainment.

A mile or so down the Arabian Gulf Road, tiny **Green Island** is connected by a pedestrian causeway. A pavement train takes passengers around the isle to a photo opportunity spot to capture the Kuwait Towers on film.

A drive south along the Arabian Gulf Road takes you past rambling palaces and residences to **Salmiya**, a favourite town with Kuwait's young crowd because of its fast-food and retail outlets. The Pyramid Mosque, perhaps unique in the Islamic world, is strangely sited on one of the town's major roundabouts.

In the Jabriya district to the west of Salmiya, the **Tariq Rajab Museum**, housed in the basement of a villa, contains a dazzling private collection of Islamic art, folk jewellery, ceramics, manuscripts, calligraphy, musical instruments, metalware and costumes—some many centuries old. Tastefully organized exhibits span the cultures of Central Asia and the Middle East.

## Towards the Desert

In the last days of the 1990–91 occupation, a corps of resistance fighters held off against Iraqi forces from two villas in **Al-Qurain**, south of Kuwait City. The houses, preserved as a **martyrs' museum**, have been left in the state in which the allied forces found them: bullet-ridden, shelled by a tank, vandalized, with blood-splattered walls and floors where resistance fighters were slain.

In the Bedouin town of **Jahra**, west of Kuwait City, is the **Red Fort**, or Palace. The spacious 19th-century fortress, actually sand-coloured, was the scene of important battles including Kuwait's struggle for independence in 1920.

**Ahmadi** is the heart of Kuwait's Burgan oil fields. The Kuwait Oil Company's Petroleum Display Centre has exhibits on oil production, drilling and pumping processes, and also shows how the company tackled the problems of environmentally devastating burning oil fields and oil lakes left in the wake of the Gulf War.

For something more light-hearted, **Entertainment City**—about 20 km (12 miles) northwest of

**Carpets and cushions galore in the market.**

Kuwait City—provides for a relaxing day with theme parks, fountains and lakes, fun-fair rides and recreational activities. Just outside Entertainment City is Kuwait's major dhow-building yard where with a bit of luck you'll see a traditional teakwood vessel under construction.

## Dining Out

Most of Kuwait's fine dining rooms are to be found in the hotels, but across the country you'll discover Arabic, Asian and European restaurants—not to mention American fast-food eateries. However, this is the perfect place to indulge in Indian food, for you will find everything from samosa stalls to comfortable restaurants serving delicious food from every region of India. The Kuwaitis adore buffets, where they can sample a bit of everything. You can order a serving of filling appetizers *(mezze)* which are often enough to make a meal on their own.

## Shopping

Here you can choose between glitzy malls and bazaars selling everything from pigeons and pulses to sandals and spices. The chic Salhiya complex, an annexe to the Méridien Hotel, houses the country's finest shops with luxury goods from around the world. But Al-Khaleejia, Al-Muthanna and a dozen other shopping centres in Kuwait offer wide ranges of merchandise, too.

Amble through the markets with their stalls of fresh produce, the glittering gold souk and the bazaar where Bedouin women sell both traditional and more contemporary household wares. Jewellery and textiles are competitively priced, and you'll soon pick up haggling skills. In the gold souk, the precious metal is sold at 18–22 carats in Arabic and Indian heavyweight styles or in more delicate European designs. Also see the women's souk *(souk hareem)*, the Abbasiya souk , and the Al-Jouma souk (the name means Friday Market, but it's also open Wednesdays and Thursdays), where treasure hunters will find carpets, rugs, old brass and copperware in a flea-market ambiance.

# PRACTICAL INFORMATION

**Business hours**. The local weekend is Friday and Saturday. Banks open 8 a.m.–1 p.m and 5p.m.–7p.m. Shops usually open weekdays 9.30 a.m.– 1.30 p.m. and 4.30–10 p.m. Government offices open Sunday to Thursday 8 a.m.–1.30 p.m. Hours are reduced during Ramadan.

**Clothing**. Wear light, airy cottons when out and about. But if dining in an elegant restaurant, you might choose to dress up a bit in air-conditioned comfort. Don't forget that you're in an Islamic country and are asked to respect local customs: women shouldn't wear mini-skirts and men should avoid wearing shorts in the street.

**Currency**. The *dinar*, abbreviated KD, is divided into 1000 *fils*: 1 KD = 1,000 *fils*. Coins range from 5 to 100 *fils*; banknotes are issued in values of 250 and 500 *fils*; KD 1 to 20.

**Electricity**. The current is 240 volts, 50 cycles AC. Most outlets are for plugs with three square pins, as in the UK.

**Health**. No vaccinations are necessary. A few weeks before your departure check with your doctor.

**Language**. Arabic is the national language; English is widely understood.

**Photography**. To avoid any unpleasantness, ask permission before taking photos of the Kuwaitis—particularly women, who tend to be camera-shy.

**Religion**. Islam is the official religion, though Christian denominations also have churches in Kuwait. During Ramadan, visitors must respect local custom by not eating, drinking or smoking in public during the day. Once the sun sets, the abstinence is over until sun-up next day. International hotels have a daytime dining room for non-Muslims.

**Social conventions**. Alcohol is prohibited. In addition, the import and use of drugs and pork products are forbidden and can lead to imprisonment. Cohabitation is illegal, as is homosexuality, as well as any shows of affection in public between men and women.

**Telephone**. The communications network is modern and efficient. The general emergency number is 777.

**Time**. GMT+3, all year round.

**Water**. The desalinated seawater is not advised for drinking: prefer bottled mineral water.

The old Bahrain Fort on the north coast near Karbabad; its last occupiers were Portuguese.

# BAHRAIN

For some, it was the biblical Garden of Eden. For others, it was the paradise that the ancients sang praises to as the Land of the Living or the Land of the Rising Sun. Bahrain is the Dilmun of the epic of Gilgamesh, an ancient Sumarian text written 4,000 years ago. The Dilmun civilization was flourishing while the rest of the world was emerging from the last stages of the Ice Age.

The desert isle—Bahrain Island is the biggest of a group of more than 30 islands—is a veritable treasure trove of remnants of this proud era: from tens of thousands of burial mounds and temples to foundations of forts and an entire 4,000-year-old village. Bahrain became a key commercial centre in ages past for the people of the region. The island gained an enviable position in Arabia for its fresh water and for the remarkable quality of its pearls, called "fish eyes" in ancient writings.

The present population of around 790,000 is mainly concentrated in the northern third of the island, which is only 50 km long and 16 km wide (30 miles by 10). A third of the population is foreign, mainly hailing from Asia, but there are also those from other Arab countries and expats from the West, most of whom have come here to work.

Gleaming office buildings and luxury hotels dominate the skyline of Manama, the capital. Most of these were constructed on land reclaimed from the sea. The surface area was increased by one-fifth thanks to land reclamation—and it's still growing. In the face of dwindling oil reserves, the nation set itself on a course of industrial diversification which includes aluminium plants as well as shipbuilding and repair yards. The new lands helped make Bahrain an important banking and commercial centre in the region.

But in modern Bahrain, the past is never very far away. Venerable residences, a thousand-year-old relic of a mosque, forts, handicraft villages and ancient ports remain, reminding Bahrainis and visitors alike of the history, culture and heritage of this country—a history spanning many millennia.

# A BRIEF HISTORY

**Early times**
The Sumerian *Epic of Gilgamesh* refers to Dilmun (paradise), now iden-
tified as Bahrain. (Gilgamesh, a semi-mythical king, is thought to have
lived around 2600 BC.) Saar village, Barbar temple, the foundations of
Bahrain Fort and burial mounds date from this era.

**8th century BC– 6th century**
Around 640 BC, the Persians conquer the island. It becomes part of the
Babylonian empire 40 years later. In the 4th century BC, two of Alexander
the Great's ships reach Bahrain, and Pliny later records that it is
renowned for its abundance of pearls. In the 4th century the Sassanian
king of Persia, Shappur II, annexes the island.

**7th–14th centuries**
Around 630 the ruler converts to Islam and many of his subjects follow
his example. In the 9th century, Bahrain, now a dependency of the
Caliphate, becomes a centre of Carmathian rule (a radical Shia sect). In
1058 a Bahraini resident, Abil-Bahloul, leads a revolt against the Car-
mathians and proclaims himself prince, but he is soon driven out by
Yahya bin Abbas, the ruler of a neighbouring state, Qatif.

**15th–17th centuries**
Oman takes the island in 1487 but it is soon liberated by the Portuguese.
They are are driven out at the beginning of the 17th century and the
island comes under Persian rule.

**18th–19th centuries**
Ahmed al-Fatih takes over Bahrain in 1783 and establishes the Al-Khalifa dynasty. In 1861 a Treaty of Perpetual Peace and Friendship is signed
with Britain. The accession of Sheikh Isa bin Ali as ruler in 1869 heralds
a period of stability and prosperity.

**20th century–present**
Oil is discovered in the 1930s. In 1971 Bahrain declares its independence; signs a new friendship treaty with Britain and becomes a member
of the United Nations. Sheikh Isa bin Salman Al-Khalifa (r.1961– 99) is
succeeded by his son Sheikh Hamad. He carries out numerous social
and political reforms, including giving women the right to vote. The
country becomes a kingdom in 2002 after a referendum. In 2006 Bahrain
and Qatar sign an agreement to build a bridge linking the two states.

# Sightseeing

## Manama

Bahrain's capital of 156,000 is a combination of sleek, modern buildings encircled by broad avenues, and narrow lanes meandering through the bazaars.

The landmark, **Bab al-Bahrain**, is the hub of the city. Designed in 1945 by Sir Charles Belgrave, Britain's political agent to the emirate, the Bab ("gate") initially served the customs operations. Today it houses the Directorate of Tourism, a shop of local handicrafts, an outdoor café and a tourist information office. It is also gateway to the **souk**, that fascinating labyrinth of streets and alleyways where shops and stalls sell anything from spices and tobacco leaves to stereos and cameras. It's a delightful place to amble, to absorb local colour, to take in the exotic scents and cacophony. Many visitors make a beeline for the gold souk on Sheikh Abdulla Avenue, an imposing three-floor granite edifice flanked by dozens of shops also selling gold, gems and precious metals in dazzling displays.

The **Heritage Centre**, a villa on Al-Khalifa Avenue, was built in the 1930s as the Law Courts. It is well worth a visit for its exhibits relating to pearl diving, fishing, falconry, modern art, music and weapons.

istockphoto.com/Lingbeek-van Kranen

**Office buildings on Bahrain Financial Harbour.**

Ideal for strollers is the **Al-Awadiya** (wind-tower district) which boasts the Gulf's largest concentration of the traditional wind-cooling structures. At the beginning of the 20th century, the first mansions began to spring up in this neighbourhood, most with expansive, palm-shaded courtyards. Sadly, many of the homes are now dilapidated, but characteristic architectural features are still evident.

Perhaps the best example of a wind-tower residence is the renovated **mansion** of the Ali Reza

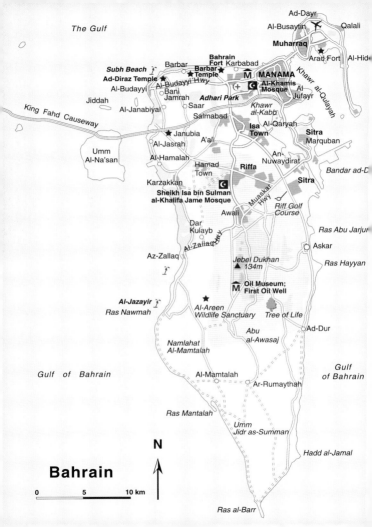

family with its grand portico and immense, leaning tower. Before modern air-conditioning came to Bahrain in the 1960s, the wind tower was an effective method of keeping cool.

Not far from the entrance to the Muharraq causeway, the **National Museum**, built in 1988, is a splendid place to enhance your knowledge of the island's culture and history. Ancient archaeological artefacts are on display, including steatite seals and pots, and glass bottles recovered from burial mounds, as well as an entire burial mound thousands of years old. Dioramas depict local customs and Bahrain's recent pre-industrial past. One of the most striking additions to the museum is a hall of dinosaurs in a setting reminiscent of *Jurassic Park*.

Located in a former technical school, built in the 1930s, the **Bahrain Craft Centre** is managed by local women. In its fascinating workshops, you can watch the manufacture of paper from palm branches, as well as wool-weaving and stained-glass, among a dozen crafts.

Among the hundreds of mosques in Bahrain, the most imposing must be the **Al-Fateh Grand Mosque** on Al-Fateh Highway. With space for 7,000 worshippers, it is the island's largest building. Two free-standing minarets soar 70 m (230 ft) heaven-

Huber/Hallberg

**In Bahrain the man's headdress is a *ghutra* and the skullcap a *keffiyeh*.**

wards while the great dome spans a diameter of 24 m (57 ft). Blending modern and traditional Islamic designs, the cavernous mosque is air-conditioned from underground ducts. Italian marble, an enormous Austrian chandelier and a giant wall-to-wall Scottish carpet complete the décor.

The restored **Al-Khamis mosque**, on Sheikh Salman Highway, is believed to be one of the oldest in the Gulf. Possibly founded in the 7th century—though a foundation stone attests to the 11th—the mosque possesses two striking minarets, which are said to date from the 15th century.

A replica of a Khamis minaret is found as part of the **Koran House** (*Beit Al-Quran*), at the eastern end of Government Avenue. This is the modern home of a priceless collection of Korans, ancient 7th- to 8th-century parchments and writing instruments, illuminated tomes, computerized Koranic print-outs, verses on grains of rice and a huge, bound Koran from India, all in distinctive styles of Arabic calligraphy.

The **Andalus** and **Sulmaniya gardens**, one opposite the other on either side of Sheikh Isa Avenue, are pleasant parks in which to relax and contemplate Arabia. Late afternoon and evening, many families head for two popular amusement parks: the **Water Garden** and **Adhari**, built round a fresh-water spring. Both have fun-park rides and entertainment to enjoy with candyfloss and a big bag of popcorn.

Golf is an increasingly popular sport in the Gulf. Bahrain's nine-hole **Golf Club** is a refreshingly green oasis as one heads into the desert.

## Island Sights

Most villages in Bahrain specialize in a handicraft or two, passed down for countless generations.

**Gems from the deep**. Clad in a thin cotton garment to protect him from jellyfish stings, a clip made of ram's horn on his nose, leather thimbles on his fingers and big toes, stone-weighted ropes tied to his feet and another rope round his waist, the pearl diver jumped into the sea and stayed under at a depth of 15 m (48 ft) for 60 seconds—until a tug at the rope warned him it was time to be hauled back up to the surface. In his bag, a dozen oysters. With luck, they would yield some of the highest quality natural pearls in the world—transformed, some believed, from raindrops caught by the mollusc during storms. After ten jumps, he could stay aboard and take a rest, warm up with a cup of coffee while another diver would take his place.

Year after year, from May to October, the pearl fishermen lived off shore over the pearl banks, their supplies ferried out by dhow. Divers and pullers would get their share of the profits, but only the merchants grew rich. Until oil was struck in 1932, pearling was the mainstay of the Bahraini economy. The industry collapsed in the 1930s, when the Japanese started to produce cultured pearls in earnest.

One thing is sure: if you buy pearls in Bahrain they will be the genuine article. Importation of the cultivated counterfeit is strictly forbidden.

Baskets, floor mats and reed chicken coops, very much a part of the household, are produced in **Karbabad** where you'll notice one or two weavers at work at the side of the road. Close by is the **Bahrain Fort**. Though the Portuguese were the last important tenants of the bulwark (some locals refer to it as the Portuguese Fort), archaeologists have discovered no fewer than six foundations on the site, the earliest dated around 2800 BC. In ancient times, the fort's position on the northern shores of Bahrain was a key vantage point for checking the advance of marauders.

If the site of Bahrain Fort was the ancient capital of Dilmun, **Barbar** is believed to be the sacred city, probably dating back to 2200 BC. In the first of three temples, a holy well dedicated to Enki, god of ground-water, was built directly over a freshwater spring. A copper bull's head was certainly one of the most remarkable finds on the site. Steatite seals with fanciful designs of warriors, animals and marriage rites, hardly more than an inch (2.5 cm) in diameter, indicate that trading went on here at the time.

In the village of **Bani Jamrah**, textile weavers use hand looms to produce colourful fabrics that local ladies find irresistible. In one working day, a weaver can fashion six metres of cloth.

istockphoto.com/Lingbeek-van Kranen

**Many believe that the Al-Khamis mosque was founded as early as the year 692.**

Small camel herds may be viewed grazing on scrub in the dunes. The camel farm at **Janubia** is a delightful place to meet those four-footed friends of the desert.

Amid the sites and spectacular sights of Bahrain, the 25-km (15-mile) **King Fahd Causeway** linking the island with Saudi Arabia is a modern engineering marvel. When completed in 1986 at a cost of $1 billion, the causeway ended 8,000 years of separation from the mainland and heralded a boom in tourism from the king-

South of Dukhan, the Tree of Life, a lone acacia or mesquite, has survived in the desert for hundreds of years.

dom and beyond. A panoramic view of the two countries' coasts is possible from a restaurant tower on the customs island at the causeway's midway point.

The causeway approach road runs past the village of **Saar**. Of all the country's archaeological sites, the dig at Saar is the most exciting, an ongoing excavation of an entire 2300 BC village, complete with temple, main street and two-room habitations. It's hoped that continuing research will unlock many of the mysteries still surrounding the period—why, for example, did the people vanish from the town around 1700 BC Ancient Saar is located about 4 m (13 ft) beneath the present ground level.

Some 170,000 **burial mounds** scattered over the northern part of the island once marked the final resting place for nobles and commoners alike from as far back as the third millennium BC. Today the tumuli number only a few tens of thousands, victims of vandalism and urbanization over the centuries. There are around 15,000 in the neighbourhood of Saar but the largest mounds, including the Royal Tombs, are near **A'ali**, a village also renowned for its potters. Much of their craft finds its way into local homes, from vases to hookah pipes.

**Riffa** has been the residence of Bahrain's ruler since 1956. You may catch a glimpse of the unostentatious palace from Sheikh Salman Highway.

The road continues south to **Awali**. This town was planned in 1934 for the foreign employees of the fledgling oil company. Today, it boasts a social club, tennis courts, a sand-dune golf course and many other creature comforts among neighbourhoods of villas with well-tended lawns. Away to the east, you can see the extensive plants of the Bahrain oil and gas industries.

A ribbon of road leads into the desert, the terrain becoming more desolate as villages slip from sight. **Jebil Dukhan** ("smoky mountain") looms over the expanse of dunes, at only 134 m (440 ft), Bahrain's highest point. Under the shadow of the *jebil* is the Gulf's first oil well, which struck black gold in 1932, an event that marked the advent of drastic changes in the economy as well as in the destiny of the entire region. The story of the industry's development over more than six decades is recounted through exhibits and photos in the nearby **oil museum**.

As you drive along the barren sandscape south of Dukhan, suddenly a great spreading tree appears on the horizon. The source of the **Tree of Life**'s water remains an enigma—there are no springs in the region. Local lore

Christine Osborne Pictures

**The Sheikh Hamad Causeway links Manama and Muharraq.**

says the gnarled mesquite is as old as the Garden of Eden, though hard-headed botanists place its age at around 400 years. Flints dating from the Stone Age were discovered in the vicinity.

A varied collection of wildlife is nurtured in the **Al-Areen Wildlife Sanctuary**, home to scores of the region's indigenous animals—and others. The Arabian oryx, virtually extinct in the wild, is a guest of honour in the reserve, but there are also zebras, iguanas, black swans, ostriches, flamingos and other animals and birds.

## Muharraq

The second-largest of Bahrain's islands, Muharraq is dominated by the sprawling international airport, inaugurated in 1932 and linked to Manama by a causeway 7.5 km (4.5 miles) long. Once a bastion against invaders and a seat of government, Muharraq still possesses many vestiges of

its past. The patrician homes of Sheikh Isa and the Siyadi family (Ahmad Siyadi was a pearl merchant) are a stone's throw from one another.

The 26-room **Sheikh Isa house** (named for the emir who ruled from 1869 to 1923), built around 1800, is divided into four areas, each with its own courtyard and well: the emir's quarters, those for the women, visitors and servants. Dating from 1900, **Ahmad Siyadi's home** is covered in artistic flourishes, both inside and out. The façade is adorned with heart-shaped crenellation, delicate symmetrical plasterwork, carved corners and an intricate portal piece. In the **dhow-building yards**, the traditional teak or mangrove seagoing vessels are constructed, still largely using non-electric tools. Having plied the seas of the region for centuries, the dhow transports both passengers and cargo as well as being used by fishermen and pearl divers.

**Arad Fort** (named after Arados, the Greek name for the island) was built in an Arabic style in the 15th century as part of a strategic network of bastions of defence against invaders. It is square, with a round tower on each corner. The Portuguese occupied the fort from 1559 to 1635. The bulwark could hold enough provisions to maintain 300 soldiers for up to three months.

# Dining Out

For centuries, Bahrain has had ties with the Indian sub-continent, so it's no wonder that Indian and Pakistani restaurants abound—whether vegetarian or so-called non-vegetarian. Rice, most often a delightfully aromatic basmati, predominates on menus, with endless variety in rich sauces. You may go ethnic, eating with your hands, scooping up spicy morsels with freshly made *naan* or *chapatti* bread. To tame mouth-searing dishes, ask for yoghurt, not water.

The traditional Arabic dishes from the Levant are also readily available, from selections of *mezze* (as appetizers, they can turn into a full meal, for it isn't always easy to know when to stop), shish-kebabs and sweet concoctions.

In addition to international cuisine, hotels usually have restaurants specializing in French, Italian, Japanese, Lebanese or Mexican dishes, among others. Live entertainment is often provided, from high-decibel disco to conventional dinner melodies.

Venturing out to some of the island's fine restaurants can be rewarding. Whether you prefer Thai or Tex-Mex, steaks or seafood, Bahraini or Spanish, homely dining in an old villa or a gastronomic experience in a palatial hall, you're sure to find something to suit your tastes. Even the well-known fast-food eateries have found their way to this desert isle, so you can catch up on hamburgers and fried chicken if such is your bent. However, do not miss out on local produce: succulent giant Gulf prawns, and grouper fish (*hammour*), best simply grilled. Buffet meals are immensely popular.

Even the most cosmopolitan coffee connoisseur is unlikely to have savoured the traditional Gulf brew. Here, coffee *(gahawah)* is prepared with the addition of cardamom and rose water. A generous pinch of saffron transforms the murky beverage into an aromatic tea-coloured drink. Locally grown dates are usually served with *gahawah*.

# Shopping

Many come to Bahrain to hunt for bargains in photographic and stereo equipment or household appliances. Others look for CDs of Gulf music. The souvenir shop in the Bab Al-Bahrain is a good starting point for an array of mementoes, from T-shirts to hope chests.

Handmade dhow models and beautifully woven baskets make attractive gifts. Easier to pack into a suitcase are reed floor mats, fabrics and local clothing, from a

Christine Osborne Pictures

robe *(thobe)* to a cape *(besht)*. Indian saris, colourful silk scarves and Omani incense are sought after by the locals. Henna, believed to strengthen hair growth, is also used here for decorating women's hands and feet for special occasions. Home cooks will delight in the range of pungent spices which can be bought from the sack.

The gold souk is an ideal area to hunt for jewellery fashioned from precious metals, pearls and gems. Bahrain is noted for the high quality of the natural pearls produced here.

Attractive greeting cards with Islamic symmetrical designs and romantic scenes of old Arabia, mounted commemorative stamps and coins and books on Bahrain are also available at the post office or speciality shops.

Though set prices may exist for common wares, haggling is customary for most items. "How much is the discount?" may be the magic phrase to bring a price down slightly.

Those who love to browse around flea markets may find some knick-knack of value at Manama's Friday market.

istockphoto.com/Clyde

**Pyramids of colour, flavour and spicy fragrance in the souk. | The pottery tradition goes back thousands of years.**

# PRACTICAL INFORMATION

**Business Hours**. The weekend is Friday and Saturday. Government offices are open 7 a.m.–2.30 p.m. Sunday to Thursday. Banks open Saturday to Thursday 8.30 a.m.–3 p.m. Shops, businesses and currency-exchange offices generally open Saturday to Thursday 8.30 a.m.–12.30 p.m. and 3.30–19.30 p.m. Stores in many shopping malls do not close until 10 p.m. Post offices are open 7.30 a.m.–7 p.m.

**Clothing**. Bahrain is Western in its approach to everyday life and, although some Bahraini women feel more comfortable in traditional *abaya*, no formal dress code is imposed. Common sense should prevail. In towns and villages, shorts are frowned upon for both women and men. Women are advised to wear dresses or blouses to cover the shoulders and back, with a modest neckline. From November to March, you'll need a sweater or jacket in the evening. From June to October, you'll be glad you packed lightweight clothing and wash-and-wear fabrics.

**Currency**. The monetary unit is the *ainar* (BD), divided into 1000 *fils*. Banknotes are in denominations from a half *dinar* to 20 *dinars*; coins from 5 to 500 *fils*. Some vendors try to give Saudi *riyals* when making change; these are usually accepted like Bahraini currency. But BD1 is equal to 10 *riyals*. If this is more arithmetic than you care to handle, politely insist on Bahraini *dinars*.

**Language**. While the official language is Arabic, English is widely understood.

**Photography**. Be sensitive about taking pictures of local people, who may be offended.

**Religion**. Islam is practised by 85% of the population. As a tolerant society, the country has several other faiths represented. During the month of Ramadan, out of respect to fasting Muslims, tourists must not eat, drink or smoke in public during daylight hours. But shops and restaurants stay open into the early hours of the morning. Every international hotel, however, will have a restaurant open during the daytime for non-Muslims.

**Time**. GMT+3 all year round.

**Water**. All drinking water should be boiled, unless you stick to bottled mineral water. Modern hotels have facilities for filtering water.

A stunning addition to the Doha skyline, the Kassem Darwish Fakhroo Centre rising high above the city.

istockphoto.com/Cowan

# QATAR

If you thought sand was just something gritty that gets into the sandwiches, you'll soon learn otherwise in Qatar. From tip to base, much of this thumb of land jutting into the emerald waters of the Arabian Gulf is desert, varying from grey dust blowing around the towns and villages, through heavy golden packed deposits easily navigated by camels, to rippling red drifts, draped and smoothed by the winds into high dunes.

Between Saudi Arabia and the United Arab Emirates, the State of Qatar is a little smaller than Northern Ireland (11,400 sq km). For hundreds of years the Qataris lived quietly from fishing and pearling, governed by the strict Islamic law, or Shari'a, based on the Koran (Quran). The capital, Doha, was hardly more than a dusty village of 12,000 inhabitants, living for the most part in tumbledown stone dwellings. Shops and bazaars huddled together in a maze of covered lanes.

Oil was discovered in 1939, and today more than four-fifths of the national income comes from oil and gas production. In just half a century the country took a tremendous leap into the industrial age. Doha has burgeoned into a glittering town of square-cut, concrete banks and agencies, hotels, embassies and ministries set along straight, broad avenues. It spreads round a wide, semicircular bay on the east coast, just above the joint of the thumb. The car is king here, and most of the efforts to beautify the city amount to monumental roundabouts adorned with symbolic studies of coffee pots, rose-water sprinklers or incense-burners, landscaped with fountains and greenery.

Though the men still wear their white robes with pride and most of the women dress modestly in black, they are hardly backward-looking; girls far outnumber boys in secondary schools and university education. Only about 20% of the 930,000 inhabitants are Qatari. The majority live in Doha, the others in a few coastal villages or the one oil refinery town of Umm Said down the coast.

# A BRIEF HISTORY

**Early times**

In the 5th century BC, Greek historian Herodotus describes the inhabitants as being originally seafaring Canaanites. In the 2nd century geographer Ptolemy places Catara (or Catra) on his map, probably locating the present-day town of Zubarah.

**7th–8th centuries**

The Qatar peninsula and surrounding region are ruled by the Al-Mundhir Arabs. Their king, Al-Mundhir ibn Sawi al-Tamimi, converts to Islam. In the 8th century Qatar is ruled by the Abbasids under the Caliph of Baghdad.

**16th–17th centuries**

Power struggles are played out in the Gulf between Portuguese, British, Dutch and French who scrap over the monopoly of trade routes to India and the Far East. The initial settlers remain on the coast living from fishing, trading and pearl diving. The nomadic Bedouins roam the interior. In 1617 Qatar comes first under Portuguese control which lasts for 21 years, then under the Turks.

**18th–19th centuries**

A tribal group including the Al-Thani family arrives in the north of Qatar during the early 18th century. They move to Doha in the middle of the 19th century under the leadership of Mohammed bin Thani. In 1867 Commander Lewis Pelly, British political resident in the Gulf, recognizes Sheikh Mohammed as the peninsula's most influential man and signs a peace agreement with him. In 1871 Sheikh Mohammed agrees with Midhat Pasha, the Turkish ruler of the region that is today Iraq, to admit an Ottoman military force into the country, and Qatar becomes a Turkish administrative district. Sheikh Qassim, Sheikh Mohammed's son, leads the way to unity of the country.

**20th century–present**

The Turks leave in 1913. Sheikh Qassim's successor Abdullah sides with Britain in World War I. In 1916 Britain and Qatar sign a protection treaty. Oil is discovered in 1939 and the first oil exported in 1949. Independence is declared on September 3, 1971, ending British sovereignty over Qatar. Sheikh Khalifa bin Hamad al-Thani, officially enthroned as amir in 1972, is deposed by his son Hamad bin Khalifa in 1995. A new constitution comes into effect in June 2005.

# Sightseeing

## Doha

Doha's palm-lined **Corniche**, a seafront promenade, sweeps grandly for 7 km (4 miles) round its bay. All the important sights are enclosed between this road and A Ring Road, the first of three highways embracing the city. East along the Corniche you can't miss the monumental oyster shell, a reminder of the country's pearl-diving roots. From there you get a good view of Doha's newest landmark, the spiral minaret of the **Kassem Darwish Fakhroo Centre** at the intersection of Grand Hamad and Abdullah bin Jassim streets. Modelled on an ancient tower in Samarra, Iraq, it stands above a multi-purpose facility that includes an Islamic Centre, a mosque, offices and department stores.

Near the intersection with Al-Muthaf Street, most of what remains of Qatar's history is gathered together in the **National Museum**. Housed in the former palace of Sheikh Abdullah bin Mohammed who ruled from 1913 to 1951, the displays are set in a labyrinth of rooms, corridors and courtyards. Particularly interesting is a Bedouin tent complete with carpets, embroidered cushions and coffee pot, looking for all the world as though the family is about to return at any minute.

There's a gallery devoted to the oil industry, and outside, beautifully restored wooden dhows floating on a lagoon. Live local fish such as sharks and stingrays can be viewed from a reasonable distance.

A walk along Jassim bin Mohammed Street towards the town centre, will take you past the landmark Clock Tower and the many-domed Grand Mosque to **Doha Fort**. Admission is free to this old building where you can buy traditional Bedouin handicrafts.

In Al-Najada Street, next to a parking lot, one of the few remaining Qatari houses with a wind tower has been restored. You can sit beneath the tower and feel the cooling effect of this ingenious ecological invention.

Opposite is the entrance to the **souk**. Venture into its alleyways for some fascinating insight into the Arabian way of life.

## North Coast

On the coast, 67 km (41 miles) north of Doha, **Al-Khor** is a small, pleasant town built round a dhow harbour. The museum, formerly a port police station, boasts archaeological artefacts from the vicinity going back several millennia. Several old watchtowers on the harbour have been restored. Established in 1963, the **Rawdat al-Faras** experimental farm is an attempt to turn the desert green

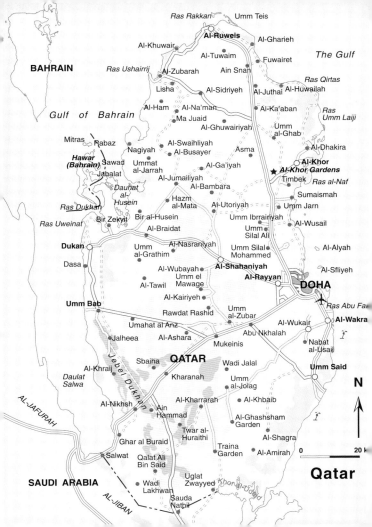

by cultivating fruits and vegetables in a hot, dry climate. There's a picnic area with restaurants and barbecue facilities at **Al-Khor Gardens**, just past the turnoff for Al-Khor from the North Road.

**Al-Ruweis**, at the northern tip of the peninsula, was once the port of call for a ferry service from Bahrain. Its clear waters are host to several varieties of coral and tropical fish. A home here is often open to visitors, to sit in the carpeted *majlis* (living room), sip sweet tea or coffee, and meet the family falcons. Women visitors are permitted to enter the ladies' part of the house where they can make acquaintance with Qatari women.

**Al-Zubarah** was Qatar's most important settlement until a century ago. Now it's virtually abandoned, visited occasionally by Qataris on falconing expeditions. The **fort**, built in 1938 as a coast-guard lookout, was transformed into a museum in 1987. A rectangular building with three round towers and a crenellated bastion, it affords sweeping views of the landscape and out over the sea, as far as Bahrain on a clear day. Several of the rooms around the courtyard display archaeological artefacts dating as far back as 5000 BC. Nearby excavations reveal walls of dwellings dating from the Abassidian era of the 8th century.

## The South

The pearl-diving centre of **Al-Wakrah** is only a 20-minute drive from Doha. One of its traditional houses near the harbour has been restored and now serves as a **museum** of marine life (Tuesday afternoons are reserved for families). There are some ruins behind it, thought to be a palace.

Beyond the city of Umm Said, hub of the steel and petrochemical industries, the desert sprawls endlessly in all directions. Only the occasional appearance of camels on the horizon relieves the infinite landscape of sand and billowing dunes. Sand-skiing and dune-driving have become popular in recent times, the skiers pulled to the top of the 40-m (130-ft) dunes by 4x4 vehicles.

After a bumpy ride southwards, with only a compass to indicate the way, you suddenly encounter the so-called inland sea of **Khor al-Udeid** appearing like a mirage. This is a saltwater inlet linked to the Gulf by a channel 7 km (4 miles) long. On the border with Saudi Arabia, Khor al-Udeid is a paradise for hang-gliders, snorkellers, swimmers, anglers and even for lazy sunbathers.

After a hard day of sun and fun at Khor al-Udeid, you can return to Doha by the coast road, less arduous than the more direct dunes route.

**Falconry is a sport held in high regard in all the Arabian peninsula.**

# Dining Out

Doha has a wide selection of restaurants specializing in Arabian, Asian and European food —and American fast-food outlets have found their way here, too. With so many Asians living in Qatar, it's no wonder that the cooking of that continent dominates, from spicy Indian dishes to wok-sautéed Far Eastern delights. But if you prefer to dine *à la française* or stick to more familiar European dishes, you'll have no problem finding the right place to eat. To venture beyond the comfortable surroundings of a hotel into a good local restaurant can be a rewarding experience.

Qataris love buffet meals, which are a wonderful way to pick and choose both well-known and exotic dishes. You could make a whole meal from *mezze* (starters) alone. The array of hot and cold appetizers is irresistible, from *tabbouleh* (cracked wheat, tomato and parsley salad), *kibbeh* (pine-nut filled meatball) and *samosa* (vegetable or meat-filled pasties) to *muktabal* (aubergine dip), *hummus* (chick pea dip) and *dolmas* (stuffed vine leaves). But save room for chicken, meat or fish kebabs; the tasty rice-casserole main dishes and the succulent whole baked lamb *(khouzi)*.

Qataris have a sweet tooth, and *uma'ali* (bread pudding) and dates and bananas in cream are among favourites.

# Shopping

Most souk merchandise can be haggled over, whether it's spices or stereos, gold or goats. Hand-worked jewellery in the gold souk is a particularly good buy.

If you're comparing prices on home appliances, textiles, perfumes, electronic goods and TV and video equipment, visit Doha's shopping centres which stock products from Europe, the United States and the Far East. Al-Saad Street is the best place to start.

If you want to take home something typical of Arabia, you might consider the characteristic Gulf coffee pots with pointed spouts, the unusual rose-water sprinklers, or slip-on sandals. Carpets, silk scarves and exotic, locally blended essences for perfumes are also sought after.

# PRACTICAL INFORMATION

**Business hours**. The weekend is Friday and Saturday. Banks, offices and post offices are in principal open from Sunday to Thursday, 8 a.m.–2 p.m. Shops open weekdays 7 a.m. or 8 a.m.–noon or 1 p.m. and 3 p.m.–7 p.m., or without interruption 7 a.m.–3 p.m. Shopping centres are usually open 9 a.m.–9 p.m.

**Climate**. From June to September it is very hot in Qatar, and also humid because of the proximity to the sea. There are occasional sand storms. In winter it can be extremely chilly at night. The most pleasant seasons for visiting are spring and autumn.

**Clothing**. Light, loose-fitting cotton garments are best in Qatar's hot climate. You can dress up for meals in some of Qatar's elegant dining rooms. In public, however, bear in mind that you're in an Islamic country where customs should be respected. Miniskirts for women and shorts for men are out of place in the streets. On the beach or at the pool, usual bathing attire is acceptable, but women cannot go topless.

**Currency**. The *riyal*, expressed as QR, is divided into 100 *dirhams*. Notes from 1 to 500 *riyals*; coins 1 to 50 *dirhams*. Currency exchanges in town generally give a more favourable rate than hotels.

**Electricity**. The current is 240 volts, 50 cycles AC. Plugs can have round or square pins; you will need an adaptor.

**Language**. While the official language is Arabic, English is widely understood.

**Photography**. Always ask permission before taking pictures of the local inhabitants, who may take offence.

**Religion**. The Qataris belong to the Wahabi sect of Islam and practise strict fundamentalism. During the month of Ramadan, out of respect to fasting Muslims, tourists must not eat, drink or smoke in public during daylight hours—though at night business is as usual. However, every international hotel will have a restaurant open during the day for non-Muslims. The date of Ramadan is fixed according to the phases of the moon.

**Time**. GMT+3 all year round.

**Water**. Drink only bottled mineral water.

Many women in the Emirates wear the black *abaya* when they go outdoors.

# UNITED ARAB EMIRATES

An ancient people in a young country is how the United Arab Emirates (UAE) sees itself. On the surface, it is the new that dominates. The ultra-modern cities are filled with luxurious hotels and amazingly high-tech skyscrapers of coloured glass and concrete, everything in mint condition. The country is criss-crossed by wide highways along which vast limousines and land-cruisers speed with nonchalant ease. The shops are crammed to the ceiling with the most up-to-date computers and cameras. This is the fabulous world of the Thousand-and-One Nights, transformed into an Arabian California.

But the visitor should beware of making hasty judgements. Look inside the limousine and you will see the driver is wearing a *dishdasha* (the traditional white robe). He might just as likely be going to a falcon hunt at a remote oasis as a business meeting at the office. And just beyond the modern skyline is the haunting grandeur of the timeless desert. The camel may have been displaced as the major mode of transport, but this is still a desert society, profoundly connected to the most famous product of that desert culture, the Koran and Islam. Indeed, it is remarkable to think that the astounding economic transformation which con-

fronts the visitor has been brought about by an essentially conservative Muslim society. For all that, the result of this blend of ancient and new is a genuinely cosmopolitan environment where, true to the ways of the Bedouin, the traveller is always welcome.

Of course, things have been smoothed along by the discovery of oil. Before it came on stream in 1962, the Gulf was struggling as one of the poorest places on earth, with Abu Dhabi being the poorest of all the sheikhdoms of the Trucial Coast (it is now the wealthiest). The coastal population lived from fishing and pearl-diving (though Dubai had long been a busy trading centre). In the interior, the Bedouins scratched a meagre living from subsistence farming and camel-herding, as well as less salubrious pursuits such as raiding and extorting money from passing caravans. Nor were matters helped by the long-standing hostilities among the various tribes in the region. Until relatively recently there have been raids and skirmishes even between the emirates themselves. The anticipation of finding more oil, together with the extremely eccentric borders that the British mapped out for the seven emirates, only added to the tension.

All the more remarkable, then, that these days the UAE counts as one of the most politically stable countries in the Middle East, as well as being a safe place to

travel in. It has existed as a self-governing state only since 1971. Following the British decision to withdraw from the Gulf, the seven emirates recognized the uncomfortable fact of being very small and very wealthy minnows in a Gulf full of sharks, and consequently joined together to form one federated country. However, each emirate is fiercely independent, and each resists moves towards increased federal power with gusto.

The UAE comprises Abu Dhabi (capital and largest of the seven, with 81 per cent of the overall territory, and the only real oil state), Dubai (the main port of entry for tourists), Umm al-Qaiwain, Sharjah, Ras al-Khaimah, Ajman and Fujairah (the only emirate without a coastline on the Gulf). Within its total area of 83,600 sq km (32,300 sq miles) there is a population of 5.4 million, of whom 75 to 85% are expatriate workers, mainly from the Indian sub-continent, South-East Asia and Europe.

The UAE's story has not been one of unhindered progress. The collapse of oil prices in the mid to late 1980s affected the smaller emirates severely as the richer ones were forced to cut back on their subsidies. The lesson learnt was that a country cannot rely on a single product forever, even one as profitable as oil.

A happy consequence of this has been the active welcoming of tourists and business travellers. The UAE has worked hard to make itself one of the most accessible places in the region

for the foreign visitor. It has all the attractions and amenities a person might want from a major holiday destination—excellent hotels, historic sights, deep-sea fishing, scuba-diving and first-rate beaches, even championship-level golf courses. Not forgetting other particularly Arabian pleasures: don't miss the chance of a desert safari, or a helicopter ride above the landscape. Better still, have a go at sand-skiing down a dune, real skiing on artificial snow, or the popular wadi-bashing: speeding through dry river-beds in four-wheel-drive vehicles. On top of all this, for the dedicated shopper there are boundless opportunities—both in the up-to-date shopping malls and the traditional souks.

istockphoto.com/Randall

# A BRIEF HISTORY

**Prehistory**

The Arabian Gulf coast comes under the influence of the civilizations of Mesopotamia and the Indus River; trade links are established. During the 3rd millennium BC, the Umm an-Nar culture flourishes.

**Early times**

The city of Mleiha trades with the whole of the peninsula and as far as Greece. In the 1st century the territory comes under Sassanid (Persian) rule. After a battle at Dibba (Fujairah) in 733, Islam is imposed.

**16th–17th centuries**

The Portuguese seize the Kingdom of Hormuz (comprising much of what is today the UAE) and control the straits between the Arabian Gulf and the Gulf of Oman. For over 100 years they tax the Gulf's lucrative trade with India and the Far East. In 1622 the British East India Company, with the Dutch and Persians, attack and eject the Portuguese from Hormuz. Around the mid-17th century the coastal communities of the lower Gulf are acquired by the imams of Oman.

**18th–19th centuries**

Decline of the Persian and Omani dynasties leads to a political vacuum that enables the Bedouin clan of the al-Qawasim to gain strength; they develop a nava power that soon eclipses colonial Britain. After several British military actions, a final invasion in 1820 leads to peace treaties concluding with 1853 Treaty of Maritime Peace in Perpetuity. The lower Gulf coast is called the Trucial Coast. In 1892 "exclusive agreements" are signed between Britain and sheikhdoms guaranteeing protection in exchange for keeping rival European powers and Russia out of the Gulf.

**20th century–present**

The British leave India in 1947, weakening their need for a military presence east of Suez. In the 1960s vast oil revenues begin to flow in. In 1968 the British announce their intention to leave the region and the UAE is formed in December 1971. The UAE, together with Oman, Qatar, Saudi Arabia, Bahrain and Kuwait, form the Gulf Cooperation Council in 1981 to strengthen the security of the region and promote economic cooperation. In the 1991 Gulf War the UAE stands firm with the UN coalition against Iraq's invasion of Kuwait. Sheikh Khalifa bin Zayed is President since 2004.

# Sightseeing

## Abu Dhabi

Crossing **Muqta Bridge**, you might be forgiven for thinking that the modern high-rise city ahead is a mirage, an illusory Arabian metropolis looming from the heat haze of the desert. Take a glance at its recent past and you may feel convinced you were right. The transformation that has taken place can only be described as magical. When British explorer Wilfred Thesiger arrived here in 1948, he could reach the level, sandy island on which Abu Dhabi stands only at low tide and on camelback. What confronted him is hard to imagine now. "A large castle dominated the small dilap-idated town which stretched along the shore. There were a few palms, and near them was a well where we watered our camels. Then we went over to the castle and sat outside the walls, waiting for the Sheikhs to wake from their afternoon slumbers." Even in the mid-1960s, the scene was not much different.

Today, however, the sheikhs have moved out to more luxuri-ous, high-tech residences and the castle is dwarfed by the town and its brand-new skyscrapers. Per-haps the very fact of its survival makes it the most remarkable of all Abu Dhabi's architectural feats. The whitewashed **Al-Husn**

**Palace**, or White Fort, is in fact the oldest structure in the city, dating from the reign of the present ruler's great-grandfather, Zayed the Great (reigned 1855–1909). It replaced an earlier fort built just after the Al-Bu Falah tribe, who form the majority of Abu Dhabi's Arab population, first settled on the island at the end of the 18th century. What brought them here was the region's most precious commodity—not oil, but water. Legend has it that a group of hunters from the Liwa Oasis were led to a freshwater well by a deer they were chasing (Abu Dhabi means "father of the gazelle"). Although the truth may be far less romantic, the ruling al-Nahyan dynasty made sure their fort was constructed over the well, as un-ambiguous an assertion of power as you could want. You are free to walk around the fort's courtyard and take advantage of your only chance to soak up the atmosphere of a bygone age in Abu Dhabi. Filled with date palms and foun-tains, it is a true oasis in the noisy, bustling city.

Within the walls of the White Fort, the **Cultural Foundation** func-tions mainly as a library and research centre, but also holds lectures and exhibitions which are open to the public. Photogra-phy seems to be particularly pop-ular, but the exhibitions may include paintings, local history

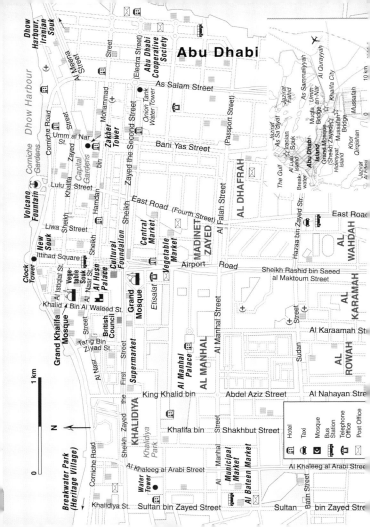

displays, manuscripts, and so on. There is also a concert hall where performances range from classical music recitals to Arabic drama. You can obtain information about the month's events from the Cultural Foundation reception desk, which is open every day except Friday.

Just across Sheikh Zayed the First Street is the **Grand Mosque**, an eye-catching mixture of Islamic architecture and white marble colonnades. You can walk through the gardens, but non-Muslims are not allowed to enter the mosque itself.

On the other side of the fort, **Ittihad Square** is adorned with amazing fountains, one representing a cannon, another a huge coffee pot. A huge shopping mall is being built on the site of the old souk nearby.

The best place to take in Abu Dhabi's modernistic façade is

**UAE and GCC.** In 1968, when Britain suddenly declared its intention to withdraw from the region within three years, the Arabian Gulf states were forced to consider their future in a dangerous world, where their much bigger neighbours nursed ancient territorial claims. It was clear that they should come together for their mutual defence, but the discussions between them were tortuous. Some of the smaller and poorer states happened to have longer histories than the big two, Abu Dhabi and Dubai, and were understandably prickly. Abu Dhabi realized it would be providing the money and expected to call the tune. Dubai rejected any idea that it should play second fiddle. In 1971, the United Arab Emirates came into being as a fairly loose federation which allows its members considerable autonomy. The ruler of Abu Dhabi, by far the largest of the emirates, with most of the oil, became President of the UAE, Dubai's ruler the Vice-President and Prime Minister. The other founding members, all much smaller, were Sharjah, Ajman, Umm Al Quwain and Fujairah. Ras Al Khaimah joined two months later. Qatar and Bahrain decided against joining. Abu Dhabi is the seat of the federal government, Dubai the commercial centre. The historic rivalry between the two towns continues, but since the formation of the UAE it has been directed to productive ends.

The 1979 revolution in Iran and the Iraq-Iran War of 1980–88 increased the feeling of insecurity in the region. The UAE joined with the other states of the Arabian peninsula (Saudi Arabia, Oman, Qatar, Bahrain and Kuwait) to form the Gulf Cooperation Council (GCC) for their mutual security.

The new Sheikh Zayed Bin Sultan Al-Nahyan Mosque, named in honour of the father of the present ruler.

along the **Corniche**, a scenic promenade which stretches along the lagoon. Better still, look down on the waterfront from the 29th floor of the Hilton Baynunah Hotel, one of the tallest buildings in Abu Dhabi, as you sip on fresh juice.

Across the lagoon on a thin arm of land is **Breakwater Park**, a favourite place for watching the sunset and enjoying the breeze. Visit the **Heritage Village**, the replica of a traditional village complete with mosque, Bedouin camp and fort (which houses an interesting museum).

At the other end of the Corniche, near the Free Port, you can investigate some bargain basement goods brought over from Iran by dhow (the traditional Arabian sailing boat), and sold in the **Iranian Souk**. A short stroll away, you'll see a number of dhows tied up near the fish market.

Before leaving town, don't miss the new and awe-inspiring **Grand Mosque Sheik Zayed Bin Sultan Al-Nahyan**: it has space enough for 40,000 worshippers beneath its domes. Its four minarets are 104 m (341 ft) high.

North of the centre, **Saadiyyat Island**, or the Island of Happiness, is being developed as a gigantic leisure centre with several museums, including a Guggenheim designed by Frank Gehry and a Louvre by Jean Nouvel, as well as a New York university campus.

**Umm an-Nar.** The settlement of Abu Dhabi may be relatively recent, but some 4,000 years ago the area was the centre of a flourishing trading culture. In 1959 a team of Danish archaeologists discovered the remains of a Bronze Age port on the nearby island of Umm an-Nar. Copper mined in the Hajar mountains was exported through here to the ancient Sumerian and other Mesopotamian civilizations. The Umm an-Nar culture extended deep into the interior of the country and lasted for centuries.

Just to the south of the city, on the road leading to the airport, the **Women's Craft Centre** exhibits and sells traditional woven fabrics, as well as other products of centuries-old crafts.

## Al-Ain

The only big city in the interior of the UAE, 160 km (100 miles) to the southeast of Abu Dhabi, Al-Ain lies the foothills of the Hajar mountains. By the 10th century it was a major centre for trade on Arabia's caravan routes. In the 18th century it was briefly absorbed into the fledgling first Saudi Arabian empire, but this state soon disintegrated. A military invasion by the Saudis in the 1950s was repelled by Sheikh

Zayed, then governor of Al-Ain, who led a Bedouin force in conjunction with the Trucial Oman Scouts under British officers. Since 1966, the oasis, historically called Buraimi, has been divided, with Al Ain on the Emirates side and Buraimi proper on the Omani side. The two are separated by a large palm grove irrigated by a complex system of canals *(falaj)*.

The most spectacular archaeological site connected with the Umm an-Nar culture has been excavated at Al-Ain and can be seen in the **Hili Gardens**, a popular municipal park. Picnicking families and strolling couples stroll around near the remarkable **Round Tomb** dating from 2300 to 2200 BC. Look for the poignant carving of two people holding hands beneath a couple of giant oryxes.

The antelopes, with their fabulous curved horns, are one of the symbols of Arabia, but by the early 1970s they were virtually extinct. One positive aspect of Abu Dhabi's new-found wealth was the funding of an intensive effort to save the species. At the Al-Ain **zoo** you can witness the result: the largest collection of Arabian oryxes in the world. Some have even been reintroduced into the wild. The zoo also contains a varied collection of other animals, including houbaras (Arabian bustards), lions, gazelles and hippos.

**Black Gold.** Oil was first discovered in the Middle East—in Iran and Iraq—before World War I. After 1918, the Great Powers swooped on Arabia like hawks and snapped up prospecting concessions throughout the region. The impoverished sheikhs were only too happy for the cash: in 1933, Ibn Saud of Saudi Arabia haggled for £50,000 from Standard Oil against future royalties. The Abu Dhabi economy at this time was based on fishing and pearl-diving. Following the collapse of the wild pearl market in the 1930s, Sheikh Shakhbut (reigning 1928–1966) granted a concession to the British-owned Iraq Petroleum Company, and later, after the war, to an Anglo-French consortium. It was the latter who discovered oil off-shore in 1958. With a population of only 15,000 at the time, it was apparent that the nation was destined for great wealth. Sheikh Zayed bin Sultan al-Nahyan, father of the present ruler Sheikh Khalifa bin Zayed, assured this outcome by forming the Abu Dhabi National Oil Company (ADNOC) and nationalizing the earlier concessions. Abu Dhabi's oil reserves are good for at least another hundred years at current extraction rates, and its natural gas reserves are vast, so the party should last for some time yet.

Al-Ain's **museum** pulls together under one roof the complex historical—and prehistorical—elements of the emirate. It contains many of the smaller artefacts found at Umm an-Nar, Hili, Jebel Hafit and other archaeological sites, such as Bronze Age weapons, jewellery and pottery. The informative explanatory labels and wall posters are in English as well as Arabic. There's an ethnographical display which concentrates on the country's proud Bedouin tradition: clothing, silver jewellery, weapons, and so on.

The 18th-century **Eastern Fort**, immediately opposite the museum, was the birthplace of Sheikh Zayed, ruler of Abu Dhabi for 38 years until his death in 2004. Beautiful doors are set in its walls, which enclose a few traditional buildings such as a Bedouin tent and a reed house. In the side rooms, a collection of old photographs gives an idea of the town as it used to be. The large new building in the style of a fort a few hundred yards from the museum is the **livestock souk**. This attracts buyers from all over southern UAE and northern Oman. To catch the best of the trading action be there early.

The oasis is dotted with numerous forts, mostly dating from the 19th or early 20th century, reflecting its historic sig-

Bernard Joliat

Claude Hervé-Bazin

On the Round Tomb in the Hili Gardens, a couple linked together since the 3rd millennium BC. | Al-Khandaq fort on the Omani side of the border would make a splendid model for a sandcastle.

nificance as a vital watering hole at an important desert crossroads. Do not miss the superb **Jahili fort** (1898) with its round tower and four levels of crenellations. **Al-Muwaiji** and **Murabba'a** are more recent but also worth a visit.

Two of the most handsome forts are on the Omani side of the border; you just have to show your passport to cross over. Only 500 m from the Hili border control, the **Al-Khandaq fort** is worth seeking out. It's at least 250 years old, but restored to a pristine finish and very photogenic. Climb up to one of the turrets and you will enjoy an excellent view of the Omani part of the oasis. Close by is a small and picturesque souk with fruit and vegetable stalls. Past the covered market is the **Al-Hilla** fort, recently restored and very forbidding-looking with its different levels of defences and crenellations.

Without doubt, though, the best souk on either side of the border is the one where you are least likely to buy anything. Back in Al-Ain the colourful **camel market**, open from early morning till around midday, is not to be missed. It is a glimpse of the old, Bedouin Arabia where, before the advent of the four-wheel-drive, the dromedary held sway. The Bedouin called them *Ata Allah*, or "Gift of God". They provided transport, milk, food, and their hair and hide became the raw material for household goods— even their shoulder blades were used as slates for schoolchildren to write on. The camel still has a part to play in the modern world, as the hard bargaining at the market demonstrates.

For light relief, there's always **Hili Fun City**. Called, rather optimistically, the Disneyland of the Middle East, the Gulf's largest theme park can offer a roller-coaster, a Dynamic Motion Theatre and an ice skating rink among its many attractions. The park is closed all day Saturday.

Located to the south of Al-Ain, **Jebel Hafit** (Mount Hafit) is one of the highest points in the UAE. The road to the summit winds upwards for 14 km (9 miles), and when you finally reach the top you are truly in the heavens. The views from here are particularly breathtaking because Jebel Hafit is in fact an enormous rock from the Hajar mountain range set adrift in a vast desert plain. And, looking west across to the Rub al-Khali, the Empty Quarter, there's nothing but the desert between you and Riyad, which lies more than 600 km (nearly 400 miles) away.

For a closer brush with the Empty Quarter head out to the **Liwa Oasis**, which stands on its very edge. This was the home of the emirate's dominant Al-Bu Falah tribe before they moved to Abu Dhabi (the ruling family are descendants). The oasis is near Abu Dhabi's Western Desert area, which contains most of its oilfields. For obvious reasons the authorities are very tight on security here—be careful where you point your camera. In reality, Liwa is a chain of some 30 small oases spreading out along an arc dotted with separate villages. It is the centre point of a huge project which aims at greening the desert; some of the plantations cover 200 sq km (77 sq miles). The high sand dunes around Liwa are famous for their dramatic beauty and once seen are not soon forgotten. Contemplating the vast, hypnotic sweep of the desert here, it is possible to understand Lawrence of Arabia's view that "this cruel land can cast a spell no temperate clime can match".

## Dubai

Glittering city and booming holiday destination, Dubai is the commercial and communications hub of the United Arab Emirates (UAE), and its largest population centre. With an area of 3,900 sq km (1510 sq miles) it is much smaller than Abu Dhabi, but larger than any of the other emirates. More than three-quarters of Dubai's population of over 1 million are expatriate workers, hailing from the Indian sub-continent, South-East Asia, elsewhere in the Middle East, and Europe.

As long ago as 1580, an Italian traveller reported that Dubai was a prosperous pearling and fishing community. It was much the same at the beginning of the 20th century, when over 300 pearl-diving dhows were stationed in Dubai's Creek. Since the 1830s Dubai has been ruled by the Al-

istockphoto.com/elefante

**Dubai by night and its sparkling marina towers.**

Maktoum family, which has had the good fortune in each generation to produce a leader of great business sense and political acumen. They created the right environment for trade, turning a blind eye to smuggling in the early days, and the port became the Gulf's chief trans-shipment centre for consumer goods. Later, oil was discovered but in limited quantities; less than 10 per cent of the emirate's wealth comes from petroleum exports while it handles over 70 per cent of the UAE's non-oil trade. Dubai's expansion continues to be driven by generous spending on infrastructure. Its airport is the region's busiest and its airline, Emirates, as well as being one of the fastest-growing in the world, is recognized as one of the best.

The idea of Dubai as a leisure destination is quite recent. The attractions of unlimited winter sunshine and warm water can't be

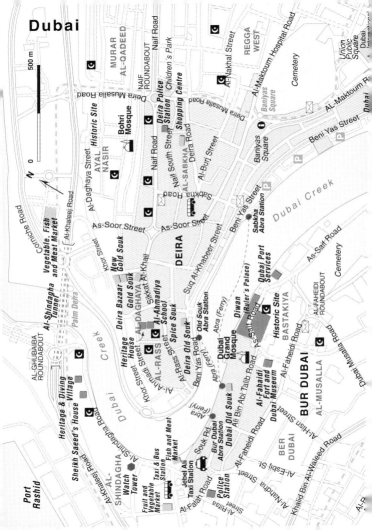

# Dubai

500 m

MURAR
AL-QADEED

Naif Road

REGGA
WEST

NAIF
ROUNDABOUT

Children's Park

Deira Musalla Road

AYAL
NASIR

Bohri
Mosque

Al-Nakhal Street

Deira Police
Station

Al-Maktoum Hospital Road

AL-MAKTOUM R

Cemetery

Shopping
Centre

Deira Road

Al-Daghaya Street

Naif South Street

Naif Road

AL-SABKHA

Al-Burj Street

Baniyas
Square

AL-MAKTOUM RD

Beni Yas Street

As-Soor Street

As-Soor Street

Sabkha Road

Baniyas
Square

DEIRA

Beni Yas Street

Dubai Creek

Khor Street

Khor Street

New
Gold Souk

Sikkat Al-Khail

Suq Al-Khabeer Street

Sabkha
Abra Station

As-Saif Road

Cemetery

Corniche Road

Deira Bazaar
Gold Souk

Al-Ahmadiya
School

Dubai Port
Services

Al-Khaleej Road

Vegetable, Fish
and Meat Market

AL-
DAGHAYA

Spice Souk

Old Souk
Abra Station

Diwan
(Ruler's Palace)

AL-FAHEIDI
ROUNDABOUT

Al-Shindagha
Tunnel

Heritage
House

Deira Old Souk

Abra (Ferry)

Historic Site

BASTAKIYA

Palm Deira

AL-RASS

Al-Rass Street

Deira Old Souk

Abra (Ferry)

Dubai
Grand
Mosque

As-Saif Road

Al-Faheidi Road

AL-GHUBAIBA
ROUNDABOUT

Creek

Khor Street

Al-Ahmadi Street

Beni Yas Road

Abra (Ferry)

Dubai Museum

Al-Faheidi
Fort and

Al Bin Abi Talib Road

BUR DUBAI

Dubai Creek

Heritage & Diving
Village

Watch
Tower

Bur Dubai
Abra Station

Dubai Musalla Road

Sheikh Saeed's House

AL-
SHINDAGHA

Al-Khaleej Road

Al-Shindagha Road

Souk Rd

Fish and Meat
Market

Bur Dubai
Dubai Old Souk

AL-MUSALLA

Al-Hisn Street

Port
Rashid

Fruit and
Vegetable
Market

Taxi & Bus
Station

Jebel Ali
Taxi Station

Police
Station

BER
DUBAI

Al-Nahda Street

Al-Falah Road

Al-Ritfaa
Street

Al-Esbil St.

Al-Waleed Road

Khalid Bin Al-Waleed Road

AL-P

denied, but it needed a decision from the top before tourism could take off. That came at the end of the 1980s. The following decade brought a flurry of ever more ambitious projects and breathtaking architecture, such as the landmark Burj al-Arab Hotel, built to resemble a dhow's billowing sail. Even more daring and extravagant is the work-in-progress highest tower in the world (its actual height is still kept secret), artificial archipelagos in the form of palm trees, a map of the world, a solar system and more, where thousands of luxury villas, all with private beaches, were snapped up within days of their release on the market.

Modern Dubai spreads far along the coast, but its historic heart is still the **Creek**. Winding inland from the Gulf for about 10 km (6 miles), this sheltered waterway divides **Bur Dubai**, the old town, from **Deira** on the opposite, northeastern, bank. The serpentine curves of the Creek provide the picturesque setting for one of the great sights of the UAE, rows of teak-built trading dhows double- and triple-parked along the Deira side. Now powered by motor rather than sail, they carry goods to and from other parts of the Middle East and travel as far as India and East Africa. The waterfront hums with the excitement of trade; it is crammed with incredibly diverse cargoes. American refrigerators and Korean electronics are piled up on the quayside next to stacks of plastic garden chairs, sacks of rice and even the occasional spiral staircase bound for who-knows-where. Contributing to the general cacophony are the *abras*, or water taxis, which criss-cross the Creek until late at night. Passengers sit back to back on a central bench, and when the boat is full it can depart. This never takes long, and the *abra* is by far the most enjoyable and easiest way to make the crossing. If you want a tour of the Creek, there is no difficulty in hiring a whole *abra* by the hour. Special sunset tours with or without dinner can be arranged through hotels and tourist companies.

The inland end of the Creek, a large shallow lagoon, is a wildlife sanctuary, used by thousands of migrating birds and a flock of a thousand resident flamingos.

Dubai's reputation for trade can soon be put to the test in the **souks** of Deira; wherever you look there are bargains to be had. Shopping expeditions are even more fun in the cool of the evening, when dull lanes become transformed into dazzling labyrinths filled with multinational crowds and the sounds of fevered deal-making. Don't be shy—haggling is virtually obligatory. The

# NO LIMITS

Dubai's planners have now gone much further than their first ambitious concept, three huge artificial islands made of sand dredged up from the bottom of the gulf, each shaped like a branching palm tree protected by a crescent. The Palm Islands, big enough for 80 hotels, shopping and entertainment centres, yacht marinas and thousands of villas, were begun in 2001, with the third island to be completed in 2014. Many of the villas were sold before construction began, a high proportion to foreigners, who have only recently allowed to buy property in the emirate.

Other projects planned or already underway are even more dazzling. A group of islands called The World has been built off the coast of Jumeirah. Together, they resemble a map of the continents consisting of 250 to 300 islets, separated by canals. They are divided into four categories: private homes, estate homes, resorts and communities. But the world is not big enough for Dubai—the Solar System and the Universe are in the works. When it is completed, Burj Dubai on Sheikh Zayed Road will be the highest building on earth, but it will eventually be overtaken by Al Burj further west along the new crescent-moon shaped Dubai Waterfront.

Dubailand, a city emerging from the desert at the edge of town, comprises theme parks, Olympic-standard sports facilities, a Snow Dome with ski runs, shopping malls and residential areas built around replicas of seven "wonders of the world". To cater to all the consumers visiting this artificial paradise, Al Maktum airport and Jebel Ali harbour, planned for 2013, will be the biggest of their kind in the world.

istockphoto.com/Yousuf

narrow corridors of the spice souk are especially enjoyable to stroll along, but there are also souks specializing in perfumes, textiles, leather, clothing, kitchen ware, vegetables, meat and fish. Most famous of all is the **gold souk**, where, in its hundreds of little shops, all that glitters is definitely gold. For the best electrical goods, take a look around Baniyas Square at the Al-Sabkha Road end.

**Heritage House** was built in 1890 for a rich Iranian merchant. It has been restored and opened to the public in 2000. Behind it is the Al-Ahmadiya school, the oldest in Dubai (1912), where the sheikhs were students. Slide shows illustrate their daily lives. On the Dubai side, near the *abra* dock, the **old souk** is less frenetic than its Deira counterparts, but atmospheric nonetheless. The **Grand Mosque**, restored in 1998, has nine large domes, dozens of smaller ones and the city's tallest minaret, at 70 m.

Nearby is the imposing **Ruler's Office**, with decorative traditional rooftop wind towers. But for a taste of the genuine "old" Dubai, carry on a short distance along the Creek to the **Bastakiya** district. Many of its buildings were once the houses of Iranian merchants from Bastak and dating from around the first decade of the 20th century. Their square wind towers were an early and surprisingly effective form of air-conditioning: the open vents funnelled any available breeze into the rooms below. Wet mats could be hung in the path of the air flow to cool it by evaporation. Bastakiya is now a prized conservation area; some of the houses are open for visits.

Opposite the mosque, the **Al-Fahaidi Fort**, built in the late 18th century, originally served to protect the Creek from foreign invaders. It has acted as both palace to the ruling sheikhs and Dubai's seat of government. It has housed the **Dubai Museum** since 1971. In the courtyard is a *kaimah*, or palmfrond house, common throughout the region up to the 1950s. An excellent exhibition showing Dubai's history has been installed beneath the fort. There is a waxwork tableau of life in the 1950s, information on the ecology and wildlife of the desert, and the chance to see inside a Bedouin black tent. In the archaeological display at the end of the museum, look out for the two graves from the Qusais tombs, 3000–3500 years old, and the bronze, steatite and ceramic artefacts found there. The Al-Qusais site, 13 km (8 miles) northeast of Dubai, is open to the public.

Near the mouth of the Creek, the Shinghada district, where Dubai began, is undergoing

hemis.fr/Renault

Huber/Mackie

restoration. A fine building in the traditional style, **Sheikh Saeed's House** was built in the late 19th century. Sheikh Saeed al Maktoum was the present ruler's grandfather and lived here until his death in 1958. An extensive renovation programme has carefully restored the house to its former glory. Made from blocks of coral, lime and plaster, it is classically proportioned with an inner courtyard, windtowers and finely carved doors and windows. The house now contains a museum of ancient documents. The old photographs showing the radical transformation of Dubai must be seen to be believed. A little further away, the **Heritage and Diving Village** is a kind of mini-souk with traditional architecture.

Dubai's architecture goes far beyond the traditional. For an idea of the latest creations, go to the World Trade Center district in the west. The two **Emirates Towers**, at 350 m (1,150 ft), were once the tallest buildings in the Middle East, but behind them is the new **Burj Dubai,** destined to reach at least 750 m (2,460 ft).

As Dubai expanded beyond the vicinity of the Creek, it was

**Dubai's hotels are among the most spectacular in the world, and Burj Al-Arab is no exception. | You'll still see the traditional side of Dubai.**

natural to develop along the coast to the southwest. And when the ruling family decided to encourage tourism, this was where the beach resorts sprang up. Sailing, wind-surfing, jet ski and scuba-diving are among the many water-based activities.

One of the tallest hotels in the world, the splendid **Burj Al-Arab**, 321 m (1054 ft) high, stands on its own artificial island, looking like a great white sail rising out of the blue waters of the Gulf. Its counterpart on shore is the wave-shaped Jumeirah Beach. Next to it on the waterfront, **Wild Wadi** claims to be the biggest and best waterpark in the Middle East. Many of its rides and water features were designed specially, based on characters from Arabian legends. However, the traditions of Islamic architecture have not been forgotten in the emirate's building explosion. The **Jumeirah Mosque** is built of sand-coloured stone in Fatimid style; its twin minarets and majestic dome show up best in the evening, when it is floodlit. It's the only mosque in Dubai that's open to non-Muslims; guided tours take place four times a week, in the mornings.

Do not miss the shopping centres; they are almost on a par with local museums! The **Mercato**, in Jumeirah, is built in Italian Renaissance style. At Jebel Ali, the superb **Ibn Battuta Mall** takes its inspiration from the travels of the famous 14th-century Arab explorer. Even more amazing is the **Mall of the Emirates** with five indoor ski runs created by Ski Dubai.

Take a trip out to the mountain village of **Hatta**, set in a little pocket of Dubai almost surrounded by Omani territory. On the road to Hatta the sand of the dunes on the regs and ergs turns deep red: the effect of iron ore from the Hajar Mountains.

With two watchtowers, the Hatta Heritage Village contains a restored 200-year-old settlement. The fort, which was the residence of the *wali* (administrator) has walls 4.50 m thick. Each of the houses contains a different exhibit (folklore, palm cultivation, and so on). The Juma Friday mosque in a palm grove is also worth visiting.

## Sharjah

Bastion of the Qawasim, the powerful seafaring dynasty that reigned over the southern shore of the Gulf in the 18th century, Sharjah has a turbulent past. Throughout the 19th century it was Dubai's main trade rival, though its position was increasingly eclipsed by its neighbour's canny business manoeuvres. Nevertheless, it was here that the British chose to locate the first airport of any consideration in the Gulf when, in 1932, Imperial Airways began using it as a staging post for its Asian routes. In the 1950s it was the site of a Royal Air Force base and today it remains the UAE's biggest handler of air-cargo. The low point came in the 1950s and 60s. While Dubai's Creek was being dredged and improved, Sharjah's harbour was negligently allowed to silt up. And as oil-rich Abu Dhabi gained political ascendancy among the emirates, Sharjah had to wait until 1974 for its first drop of oil to be discovered. The infighting among the ruling al-Qasimi family can't have helped much. There was an attempted coup in 1972 and the latest quarrel was in 1987, when the ruler's brother tried to overthrow him. With the weight of the UAE's Supreme Council on his side though, Sheikh Sultan was soon restored to power.

As anyone looking at the city today can see, Sharjah has survived and flourished. Hoping to cash in on the overspill from Dubai's economic success, Sharjah underwent a massive hotel-building boom. The **Central Market**, or New Souk, is a manifestation of this optimism. A civic building project on the grand scale, it looks disconcertingly like a row of connected oriental "cathedrals" with blue domes topped by square towers. In fact these are working wind towers, which

achieve a welcome degree of coolness inside. This is very much a modern shopping mall, and if your taste in souks runs more to the orderly than to the riotous, this is the one to head for. It is also reputed to have some of the best bargains in the Emirates. On the upper floors in particular, you can find a whole host of shops selling Persian carpets, silverware, jewellery and that symbol of gracious Arabian living, the long-necked coffee pot.

Across Al-Ittihad Square, the **King Faisal Mosque** counterbalances the more worldly attractions of the souk. It can accommodate up to 3,000 worshippers at a time.

Making great efforts in the tourist industry, Sharjah has drawn up a programme to display its heritage and to encourage culture and the arts: there are no fewer than 17 museums, where visitors are welcomed with coffee and dates. It was designated the cultural capital of the Arab world by UNESCO in 1998.

In the heart of the old town, Al-Gharb, just back from the Corniche, a block of houses has been restored. The **Heritage Museum** is housed in several buildings with wind towers. The main one, in the Al-Naboodah house, displays costumes, jewellery and other items of daily life that reveal some of the atmosphere of past times.

Next door, the **old souk** has been so extensively restored that it has the cleaned-up air of a museum piece. But its narrow, covered lanes are still a wonderful place to walk around for their atmospheric evocation of a past way of life in Arabia.

The **Museum of Islamic Art** exhibits a splendidly eclectic collection of works from all over the Muslim world: ancient coins, pottery, manuscripts, scientific instruments, maps, weapons and so on.

Several other museums are set up beneath the old palm timbers of the district. One is dedicated to its restoration, another to traditional jewellery, yet another to costumes and cosmetics, without forgetting the **Game House**, where you can see toy dromedaries made from starfish. In the **Maritime Museum**, old boats and exhibitions illustrate the pearling industry and trade.

A short walk away, **Al-Hisn fort** was long the residence of the emirs of Sharjah; it was built in 1820, destroyed in 1969 and rebuilt exactly like the original.

The neighbouring Arts district (Shuwaiheen) includes the big **Sharjah Art Museum** (mostly canvases and orientalist watercolours from the 18th century to the present day), as well as several art galleries and institutes. Stop for a break in the Arts Café.

South of town, the state-of-the-art **Archaeological Museum** covers the entire period from the origins to the advent of Islam. Some remarkable objects were discovered in the city of Mleiha—moulds for minting coins, gold ornaments from a horse buried with its owner, Rhodian amphoras, Yemeni marble pots, and so on. In each room, films put the discoveries into perspective.

In view of Sharjah's new role as a beach resort, a number of hotels have been built all along the sandy shore in the directions of Dubai and Ajman, and especially on the banks of the two artificial lagoons, Khaled and Al Khan.

For an enjoyable excursion, head out to the **Desert Park** on the Sharjah to Dhaid road, 25 km (15 miles) from town and just beyond the airport. The park's gleaming **Museum of Natural History** makes excellent use of graphics, videos and models and has an underlying ecological theme throughout. You can take a journey through time, right from its beginnings with an exploration of the "Big Bang", and you'll also learn a great deal about desert geography and geology, as well as its history, stretching back to the earliest moments of the peninsula. Given the museum's location, it is hardly surprising that the desert should be an important

Homes were air-conditioned by wind towers, letting warm air out and cool air in.

subject here. But it's rather strange to reflect that Arabia once resembled the African savannah, covered by lush jungle and supporting animals such as zebras and hippos.

Next to the Breeding Centre for endangered wildlife, the **Arabian Wildlife Center** aims to present and safeguard the animals native to the Arabic peninsula. Many are threatened with extinction, like the superb Arabian leopard.

## Ajman

Ajman is the smallest of the seven emirates, a mere 260 sq km (100 sq miles) in area. The first recognition that this tiny settlement was an independent sheikhdom came in 1820 when the British forced the ruler to sign the General Treaty of Peace along with all the other Gulf leaders. Since then it has managed to carve out an identity for itself as a famous dhow-building centre— even today the boatyards along the waterfront are a popular destination for visitors wishing to see the old skills still in use. Ajman has not been blessed with any oil discoveries but has benefited from being part of a federation where revenues from oil, primarily from Abu Dhabi's vast fields, are used to support poorer states. Its enclave at Masfut in the Hajar Mountains, however, yields high-grade marble as well as a vital

resource for modern tourism, mineral water.

Ajman's well-restored **fort** should not be missed. It is one of the finest old forts along the Gulf and also contains a good museum. Built in the second half of the 18th century, it reflects a mixture of architectural styles, from the Portuguese-influenced bastions to the traditional Arabian wind towers. Ajman's rulers lived here until 1970 when it became the local police headquarters. In 1981 the new ruler, Humaid V, gave instructions for it to be converted into a museum dedicated to Ajman's cultural heritage. In the forecourt there are a couple of examples of the traditional boats built in Ajman, including a *sam'aa*, or pearling dhow, plus an old-style palm-branch house. The museum shop on the left as you enter sells local handicrafts as well as a useful museum guide.

The museum has gone into waxwork displays in a big way. They are used to demonstrate costumes, women's crafts, children's games and the old-style kitchen, and one long room is given over to a reconstruction of a typical street in the old souk. There is also an excellent collection of photographs of famous Ajmani pearl divers, whose exploits are recorded for posterity. And not to be missed is the chance to actually sit beneath a wind tower and test whether the system is really effective. Reflecting its previous incarnation, the museum also has a police exhibition with such unusual displays as a wooden punishment block, police pistols, manacles and tear-gas bombs.

If you don't mind an early start, it is worth seeing the food **souks** on the waterfront. The fish souk is particularly lively and at its best before 9 a.m. when the fishermen have just brought in the day's catch. Not far away is where they dock their boats. These line the jetty and, covered in their complicated web of fishing nets, look very photogenic.

In the Sharjah direction, the coast is hemmed by a nice beach with shelters providing welcome shade.

## Umm al-Qaiwain

The little fishing village of Umm al-Qaiwain was built on the tip of a thin spit of land which protrudes from the Gulf coastline like a crooked finger. In the past, an important source of income for the emirate, which does not have petrol, was the manufacture and sale of brightly coloured postage stamps. One couldn't post anything with them, though, as they were purely for philatelists with a taste for the exotic. Today, Umm al-Qaiwain remains a sleepy, relatively undeveloped place where you will see goats being herded through the main street and the skyscraper is unknown. This lends it considerable charm, for it is the nearest experience to what life was like in the Emirates before the oil boom.

Things weren't always been so quiet. The **old fort**, dating from the 18th century, was bombarded by the British as part of their punitive raid on the Pirate Coast. It is as imposing as any of the Gulf forts, with a row of cannons and a tank outside looking suitably martial. In the courtyard, a dhow rests beneath the palm trees. The side rooms are used to exhibit weapons, scale-model boats, pottery and bronze artefacts from the excavations at Ed-Dour, contemporary with Mleiha. Note the beautiful collection of traditional gold jewellery; some pieces are splendid examples of filigree work. On the upper floor, the *majlis* room is surrounded by balconies of carved wood.

The aquarium of the **Marine Resources Research Centre** at the tip of the peninsula, is open Sunday to Thursday 7.30 a.m. to 2 p.m. The ponds are not well kept, but you can learn to identify the main species of fish in the Gulf, and there are a few turtles.

The neighbouring beach is undergoing development; 20 km (12 miles) to the north, the

**Dreamland Aquapark** draws many holiday-makers with its wet rides, water games and wave pools. It stays open to 7 p.m. or later in summer.

Fishing is still a major part of the economy, and the emirate is an important supplier to the whole of the UAE. Walk along the harbour and you will soon encounter fishermen returning with their catch or hanging up rows of fishing nets to dry.

## Ras al-Khaimah

Like many other parts of the UAE, archaeological excavations have revealed early settlements in Ras al-Khaimah going back at least 5,000 years. But even its recorded history is a long and rich one. The origins of the city lie a few kilometres north in the ancient town of Julfar, which was a major port as far back as the 7th century and involved in a trade network that stretched to India and China. The Portuguese explorer Vasco da Gama arrived there in 1498 en route to India. He was helped by the famous Arabic navigator, Ahmed bin Majid, who came from Ras al-Khaimah and led da Gama to Calicut. Ironically, by so doing, he also assured Portuguese control of the lucrative oriental spice trade and guaranteed its ascendency over Ras al-Khaimah for the next 100 years.

During the 16th century the Portuguese built a customs house and fort and generally ran the show, but by the early 1600s the British and Dutch were in the region. With local tribes they attacked Julfar, pushing out the Portuguese and destroying their buildings. Julfar was abandoned by its Arab inhabitants in 1633 when they moved to modern Ras Al-Khaimah city.

The Al-Qasimi tribe established themselves as rulers here in 1747 (and later in Sharjah as well), controlling the Strait of Hormuz and repelling colonial powers. At the beginning of the 19th century they had a fleet of several hundred ships. This threat to British power led to the 1820 invasion and signing of the Peace Treaty between the defeated sheikhdoms and Britain. When the UAE was formed in 1971, Ras al-Khaimah initially declined to join the federation, taking a further two months to acknowledge the inevitable.

This emirate is one of the most beautiful, with spectacular mountain scenery and coastline. It is also very fertile, producing much of the country's food and earning a name as the breadbasket of the nation. Oil was discovered in commercial quantities in 1983 and Ras al-Khaimah became the fourth contributor to the UAE's fuel bonanza.

The city is divided by a lagoon, with the old town situated on the western side. The **Ras al-Khaimah fort** was built by the Persians during their brief period of rule in the early part of the 18th century. Most of what you see today, however, is no more than 100 years old, rebuilt after it was heavily bombed by the British in 1820. The museum is particularly informative on the emirate's archaeological sites. There's an excellent coin collection. In 1985, a local farm-hand found more than 120 coins while he was digging a well. They turned out to be 11th-century silver dirhams struck at the Oman mint at Sohar. Some of them have been cut—a corner was removed to give back change! Artefacts discovered at Julfar are also exhibited in the museum.

Take time to look at the Qawasim Room, whose raison d'être is to refute Britain's description of the area as the Pirate Coast. Defending their ancestors' good name, the modern Al-Qawasim (Qawasim being the plural of Qasimi) assert that the British raids had less to do with quelling piracy than maintaining Britain's monopoly of maritime trade. On the upper floor there's another chance to test the effectiveness of a wind tower.

There are several interesting places to see outside the emirate's main city, although you'll require some perseverance to reach them. Some 5 km (3 miles) to the north are the excavations at **Shimal**. Known locally as Qasr az-Zubba, Sheba's Palace, these early hilltop fortifications and ruined buildings, which overlie a pre-Islamic stronghold, have nothing to do with the famous queen (she was from Yemen, in fact). The site is the northernmost outpost of the Umm an-Nar culture (3rd millennium BC). It was still occupied during the 16th century. The hill is quite steep but the view from the top is well worth the effort.

A few kilometres north, **Rams** is where the British marines landed in 1819. A quiet seaside village, it has a very pleasant harbour which is nice for a stroll. You can't miss the old watchtowers, one of which is in the centre of the village. They obviously served their purpose—as the British came ashore, the population of Rams fled north to the hilltop fort at **Dhayah**, to the north. Dhayah has the distinction of being the last Qawasim stronghold to be taken by the British before this area became "trucial".

If all the hill-climbing proves too exhausting, head southeast inland from Ras al-Khaimah to the **Khatt Hot Springs**. It's not difficult to relax here in the warm mineral waters and enjoy the friendly atmosphere engendered among the bathers. There are separate pools for men and women.

The emirate also has one of the country's best camel racing tracks. At Digdagga, 10 km (6 miles) south of the capital, the pace can get very hot, although this usually has more to do with the reactions of the crowd than the speed of the racers.

## Fujairah

Fujairah lies entirely on the Batinah, or east coast, and is thus the only emirate without a presence on the Arabian Gulf. To compensate, it has the most spectacular scenery in the UAE. The road north from Fujairah to Dibba along the Green Coast runs between the stark, volcanic Hajar mountains and the beautiful beaches of the Gulf of Oman. Throughout the 19th century Fujairah was considered to be part of Sharjah. It wasn't until 1952 that the British government recognized it as a separate sheikhdom. Due to the eccentric arrangement of the emirates' borders, however, Sharjah still rules the port of Khor Fakkan, neatly splitting Fujairah in two.

Fujairah is a sleepy, provincial town with a fine corniche on which to enjoy the late afternoon breeze. Its purpose-built museum, opened in 1991, has an especially strong archaeological section. There are certainly plenty of ancient sites in the area for it to concentrate on, and you can see pottery, arrow-heads and vessels excavated from from tombs at Bidya (Badiyah), as well as artefacts from Bithna and Qidfa, including a container made from an ostrich egg.

From the square in front of the museum, you can easily see, 500 m to the north, the old fort, which has been nicely restored. It is one of the oldest in the emirates, dating back to 1670. To reach it, you have to go through an area of wasteland that used to be the heart of the old town; the ramparts and houses are being restored.

South of Fujairah, Khor Kalba has one of Arabia's biggest black mangrove forests and is a must for bird-watchers.

The best archaeological site to visit is at Bithna in the Hajar mountains. Beneath a corrugated iron awning is the Iron Age T-shaped tomb, a communal burial chamber discovered in 1988. The Fujairah museum has useful information on this site. Also at Bithna, an old fort provides good views across the mountain pass which it once guarded.

North along the coast, Khor Fakkan, an enclave belonging to Sharjah, is renowned for its busy port and long curving beach. The sand is quite coarse and the container port, at one end, does noth-

Half-hidden behind a thicket of palms, the old fort at Bithna guarded the route through the Hajar mountains.

Claude Hervé-Bazin

ing to enhance the scenery. The most pleasant area is in the centre, near the mosque, with lawns, palm trees and benches.

Next to the main road at **Badiyah** you can see a small, four-domed mosque, claimed as the oldest in the UAE. It was built between the 15th and 17th centuries. The interior can be visited in the company of the imam (donation welcome). It resembles a grotto with a massive central pillar supporting the ceiling. In the hills behind the mosque are two more old watchtowers, both restored.

Carry on to **Dibba** at the Oman border and you will be treated to a spectacular view of the Musandam peninsula, stretching away to the Strait of Hormuz. Dibba is a landmark for Islam in Arabia: following the victory of Muslim armies over local tribesmen in AD 633, just one year after Mohammed's death, Islam could claim control over the entire Arabian peninsula.

# Sports and Leisure

The United Arab Emirates, and Dubai in particular, offer versatile sports and leisure facilities for visitors. Magazines such as *Time Out Dubai* and *What's On* give detailed programmes of cultural entertainment. Tour operators and hotels offer many more activities: short camel rides or longer safaris with nights in a bedouin tent; sand skiing or boarding; dune driving in specially equipped four-wheel drive vehicles; expeditions to explore the mountain wadis; and flights over the Gulf, desert and mountains by helicopter, seaplane or conventional aircraft.

The large hotels all have sport clubs, fitness centres and facilities for water sports, with all the necessary equipment on hand. There are several go-kart tracks, and if you're finding the heat too much you can even go ice-skating! Dubai has two rinks and a junior ice hockey club; skates can be hired. You can also wind down in the luxury health spas, which offer many holistic therapies, ayurveda treatments, massage, aromatherapy, hydrotherapy, reflexology—everything imaginable to nurture your mind, body and soul.

## Water Sports

Water-skiing, jet-skiing, windsurfing, sailing, fishing—every water sport you can think of is provided for here, generally by private clubs or large hotels. A constant breeze, weak currents and the comfortably warm water create conditions that are perfect for beginners and experts alike. Divers can explore wrecks in the Gulf; the best place for diving is the coast off Fujairah.

## In the Desert

Just beyond the city limits, the desert begins. Among the more unusual activities you can practise here in the dunes, all year round, are sandboarding or sandskiing. You have to climb to the top of the dunes, or get a lift by camel, and glide back down again.

Another way to admire the desert landscape is to hire a four-wheel-drive land cruiser. Tackling the dunes requires practice and skill; tuition for one- or two-day courses is available. Even

**Hi-Tech Races.** It's worth turning up early to see the racing camels arrive, lean and almost delicate looking compared with working strains, and wrapped in blankets against the morning cold. The field for each race is assembled, camels and riders jostle their way to the start, the tape lifts and they're off! A typical race is 8 km (5 miles) or more and the melee of flailing legs and bobbing heads soon disappears into the distance in a cloud of dust. Paralleling the race is a four-wheel drive vehicle with a TV camera on top, relaying pictures to screens in front of the stands, while dozens of cars follow behind. Inside them are the trainers, radio units in hand, sending instructions to the robot jockeys riding the camels! Soon the throng of gangling animals rolls into view and excitement mounts until they cross the line. The remote-controlled 10-lb robot riders, with mechanical legs, arms and riding crops (sometimes just a receptor is used), were introduced in 2005 after protests by human rights groups at the traditional custom of using small boys as jockeys, secured to the saddles with Velcro. Race times have improved dramatically.

istockphoto.com/Nel

experienced drivers always travel with at least one other vehicle as it is easy to get stuck in the sand. Don't forget to take your mobile phone.

## Golf

This is one of the most popular sports in the United Arab Emirates, and several international standard courses have been conjured up from the sands as if by magic. Dubai boasts four championship-level grass golf courses, unlike many other courses in Arabia where you have to carry around a small square of astroturf from which you tee off. The Emirates Club at Jumeirah has a course designed by Colin Montgomerie, and you could almost pay a visit to the Dubai Creek Golf and Yacht Club for its club house alone. Inspired by the billowing shapes of sailing dhows, it resembles a scaled-down version of the Sydney Opera House. The courses are open to visitors and equipment can be hired.

Many of the golf clubs also have facilities for tennis and squash, and may also have a swimming pool. The Dubai Creek Golf and Yacht Club organizes deep-sea fishing trips.

## Spectator Sports

A favourite attraction for visitors is the camel racing, which takes place at Dubai, Abu Dhabi and Al

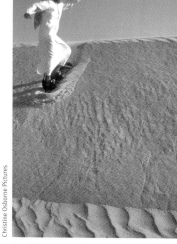

Christine Osborne Pictures

**Sand is not as slippery as snow, but snowboards are still great for dune surfing.**

Ain. The most important races are held on Fridays and Saturdays during the winter, on a track inland from Jumeirah. Don't expect any classic sprints; the participants, with their deceptively unhurried, loping style, take some time to get up a head of steam. The races start early, so aim at getting to the track before 7.30 a.m. Any spare time can be spent in the entertaining open-air market selling camel bells, beads, blankets and rugs as well as assorted souvenirs.

**Sticky Arabic pastries filled with pistachio nuts and syrup.**

Horse racing may be less exotic but it is even more popular. They are generally held twice a week from November to March and start at 7 p.m. There are generally six races, at half-hourly intervals. The Maktoum family are famous patrons of racing, and highly successful owners. Their horses fly all over the world to all the most famous races, and when they're at home, they live in air-conditioned stables and have their own huge bathing pools. The emirate itself stages the richest horse race in the world, the Dubai World Cup, held in March at the Nad al-Sheba Club, some 5 km southeast of Dubai. Night meetings at the Dubai Racing Club are particularly lively as well as pleasantly cool. The Godolphin Gallery near the racecourse displays the glittering trophies the Maktoums' horses have won around the world, with interactive video presentations.

# Dining Out

There is little that might be called an indigenous UAE cuisine. The nomadic Bedouin had a limited diet: on special occasions they might feast on goat or mutton with rice, but the staple was camel's milk and dates. The coastal Arabs, of course, had a supply of fish to vary their meals. What we know as Middle Eastern cuisine mainly comprises Lebanese, Iranian and Egyptian, available throughout the Emirates. All types of Western cooking can also be sampled, from hamburgers to the English Sunday lunch. Several good Indian restaurants are to be found in Dubai.

For a range of Arabian specialities, order a *mezze*, a selection of starters that is as filling as a main course. On one tray you will be introduced to such delights as *tabbouleh* (parsley salad with cracked wheat, tomatoes and mint), *hummus* (a chick pea and sesame seed dip), *mukta bel* (aubergine purée), *wara einab* (stuffed vine leaves with rice) and *tahini* (a dip of sesame seed paste, yoghurt and lemon). If you are still able, try a main dish such as *makbous* (spiced lamb with rice), *hareis* (long-simmered barley and tender lamb), *ghouzi* (grilled lamb or young camel stuffed with spicy rice and pine kernels), or locally caught fish or shellfish such as red snapper, kingfish, pomfret, lobster and crab. A traditional snack is *shawarma* (grilled slivers of chicken or lamb, served with salad and stuffed into a pita bread).

Popular desserts include *esh asaraya* (a type of cheesecake covered in cream) and *umm'ali* (bread pudding with cinnamon and nutmeg). The Middle East is famous for its sweet tooth and even sweeter pastries, although fruit is the usual end to a meal. The most common are dates; there are numerous kinds, varying in size, colour and sweetness.

**Drinks**

Coffee is more than just a drink, it is an expression of the culture. Business and bargaining are traditionally never done without it, and coffee houses are repositories of cordiality and conversation (and, typically, only men). Roasted and pulverized beans are brewed in small brass coffee pots and served in tiny cups. It is often flavoured with cardamom. The sugar is usually boiled at the same time and the coffee will be very sweet unless you make it clear you want it either *mazbout* (medium sweet) or *murra* (unsweetened). Let the grounds settle before drinking.

Alcoholic drinks are sold exclusively in the big Western hotel restaurants and bars. Sharjah is an exception and bans all alcohol.

# Shopping

As almost all the emirates operate as open ports with low import duties, goods from around the world appear in the shops and the souks at enticing bargain prices. At times it seems that the UAE is a vast Aladdin's cave crammed with the very latest watches, cameras, designer fashion, sportswear, perfume and cosmetics. In the souks, bargaining will be expected.

As one might expect, the UAE is a great place to buy traditional goods from the Middle East. Sharjah and Dubai are known for their excellent prices on Persian carpets (but note that US Customs bans their importation). Note that no matter how many carpets the vendor unrolls for your appraisal, you are not obliged to buy, not matter how embarrassed you may feel! Always inspect them closely before you commit yourself, looking at the number of knots per square inch, the detail of the design and the quality of the dye.

Tablecloths and robes embroidered with chain-stitched decoration in silver or gold-coloured thread are modestly priced. Every souvenir store has

an array of rosewood tables, boxes and backgammon boards inlaid with pieces of bone and mother-of-pearl. Other popular items include brass coffee sets, hand-carved wooden dhow models and various ornaments set with turquoise, lapis lazuli and other semi-precious stones. Genuine antique silver jewellery is rare these days; you will be offered more or less convincing copies of old Bedouin belts and necklaces. Many of them incorporate silver coins, including Austrian Maria-Theresia silver dollars. These too are usually replicas, with an 18th century date, but with the right quantity and purity of silver. You can also rely on the gold in Dubai's gold souk; the traders' reputation is at stake. In general, the price of the bangles, earrings and necklaces is determined by the weight of gold, with only a minimal mark-up for the workmanship. Always visit several merchants before buying, and obtain a detailed receipt. It's difficult to find genuine ancient wooden coffers these days, but you'll have no problem finding a copy. Henna, khol, incense and spices are sold in the souks.

**There's plenty to tempt you in the souks, from slippers fit for Sheherazade to brass pots and incense burners, or the inevitable *shisha*.**

# PRACTICAL INFORMATION

**Business hours**. Banks, post offices and government offices open Sunday to Thursday 9 a.m.–1 p.m. (some re-open late afternoon and Saturday mornings). With variations, shops open Sunday to Thursday 9 a.m.–1 p.m. and 4–9 p.m. or later and 5 p.m.–8 p.m. on Fridays. Souks and shopping centres are mainly open every day 10.a.m.– 11 p.m.

**Climate**. Average summer temperatures (Apr–Sept): during the day 40°C (104°F), at night 32°C (90°F). The east coast and mountain regions are cooler. During the winter months, the weather is more temperate, with desert areas becoming cold at night.

**Clothing**. Take lightweight clothing for daytime throughout the year, with a sweater or jacket needed for the more chilly winter evenings. Conservative dress in public is advisable. Sunhat, sunglasses and sun block cream are essential.

**Credit Cards**. The major cards are widely accepted, except in small businesses. Some shopkeepers may attempt to add a supplement, but this practice is illegal so make sure they don't get away with it! You can use your card to withdraw money from cash dispensers (ATMs) as long as you know your PIN.

**Currency**. The *dirham* (Dh) is divided into 100 *fils*. Coins from 10 fils to Dh 1. Notes from Dh 5 to Dh 1000.

**Electricity**. In Abu Dhabi: 220/240 V AC, 50 Hz. In the northern states, 220 V AC, 50 Hz. Plugs have 3 square pins.

**Language**. Arabic, with English widely understood.

**Photography**. Be sensitive about photographing local people, especially women. Always ask permission first. You should not take photos of airports, government buildings or military subjects.

**Religion**. Predominantly Sunni Muslim, with minorities of Ibadi and Shia Muslims. During the holy month of Ramadan, Muslims fast and refrain from smoking between sunrise and sunset. Tourists should be considerate and not eat or smoke in public. The dates of Ramadan are calculated according to the phases of the moon and change yearly.

**Telephone**. Calls within each state are free. The country code is 971.

**Time** difference. GMT + 4, all year round.

**Water**. Drink bottled mineral water.

In Oman the doorways of mosques and palaces are beautifully decorated.

Regula Reuter

# OMAN

The Arabia of myth and legend lives on in Oman: desert forts guarded by white-robed figures armed with ancient rifles and curved daggers; palm-shaded oases; the home port of Sindbad the Sailor; and a fiercely independent but hospitable, courteous people. And oil is there, too, although in modest quantities so that the income has permitted sensible development but little in the way of extravagance.

Lying along the eastern shores of the Arabian peninsula, Oman covers some 300,000 sq km (115,000 sq miles). At the far northern tip, and cut off from the rest, is the Musandam Peninsula, a beak of land pushing out into the Strait of Hormuz and occupying a strategic position overlooking the entry to the Arabian Gulf.

The coastline is at its most inviting around Salalah on the Arabian Sea in the south, and in the north between Shinas and Mutrah where it is known as the Batinah. Long, lovely beaches, feathery date palms, groves of citrus and lush fields of alfalfa embellish this curving fertile plain, backed by the towering Hajar mountains, whose peaks climb to more than 3,000 m (10,000 ft). Beyond this stone wall, the land falls away again into the endless spaces of the Arabian Desert.

Unlike the people of the interior, whose isolation made them self-reliant and aloof, the coastal dwellers have had centuries of contact with the outside world. Their ancestors sailed before the monsoon winds to trade with India and East Africa, and they carry the traces of Asian inter-marriage to this day. The people are mainly cultivators, herdsmen or fishermen, some of them still putting to sea in curious rafts of palm wood. Their traditional palm houses, barasti, built so as to get the full benefit of any sea breeze, are now mainly museum pieces, though you may spot one or two along the coast.

The Green Mountain (Jebel Akhdar), so called from the colour of the rock, is a cool, craggy

Neil Perrinjaquet

Martin Gostelow

Huber/Schmid

highland dotted with orange orchards, vineyards and walnut groves, with natural areas where flowers—roses, marigolds and tall pink hollyhocks—run riot. In Saiq, a town of roses, the petals are collected and boiled, and the liquid distilled to make rosewater, on sale throughout the country.

Inland oases support fig, peach, apricot and pomegranate trees. Water to irrigate them is brought from the mountains by the age-old falaj system of tunnels and stone channels. The supply is extremely reliable, even over long dry spells.

The west and centre of the country is a sun-beaten land of shifting sand dunes and thorn bushes, habitable only by a few Bedouin, their camels and goats, and in recent years, oil men. Animals in the more remote regions include the shy Arabian tahr, a kind of gazelle, panthers, wild cats, wolves, porcupines and rare black hedgehogs. The seas are exceptionally rich in fish, and the government is actively concerned to protect stocks from foreign fleets which would over-exploit them.

**From forts like the one at Nizwa to sumptuous mosques such as Asma Bint Alawi in Muscat and men proudly sporting their *khanjar*—Oman will leave you with vivid memories.**

South is the province of Dhofar, with another beautiful coastal plain, hemmed in by the rugged Jebel al-Qara. The often generous rainfall of the summer monsoons brings a rush of new growth, dressing the hillsides in verdant green, to the surprise of first-time visitors who come expecting desert. Frankincense, the fabled scent borne by the Three Kings, was Dhofar's most famous export for thousands of years and was even sent to the Great Temple of Babylon. Salalah is the provincial capital, with a varied mix of people including many black Omanis, the descendants of immigrants from Zanzibar.

Oman's population of around 2.7 million is growing fast, now that infant mortality has been cut to a tiny fraction of the levels of thirty years ago.

The language is Arabic, in several different dialects. Religion is almost 100 per cent Muslim, with the majority (55 per cent) belonging to the Ibadhi sect which established its separate identity as early as the 7th century. The remainder are mainly Sunnite and there are some Shia. In recent years there has been a cautious opening up to tourism, and visitors have been given the chance to discover this friendly, fascinating corner of Arabia.

**Rebirth of a Nation**. A major sea power in the Middle Ages, later a great trading empire and the first Arab state to send an ambassador to the United States, Oman had, by the mid-20th century, become an isolated backwater. Racked by internal squabbles, desperately poor, it was cut off from the outside world by its ruler, Sultan Said bin Taimur, who was dead set against development of any kind. He banned travel abroad, and severely restricted it even within Oman. His son Qaboos bin Said was allowed to go to Britain for his education but on returning home was put under virtual house arrest. When oil revenues began to flow in during the 1960s, Said refused to spend them to improve the lot of his people.

In 1970, Qaboos took over power in a bloodless coup and immediately began to make up for lost time. Within a few years, hospital beds increased from a mere 12 to over 3,000, and the number of children in school went from 900 to a quarter of a million (primary enrolment is now over 80 per cent). Then, there were only 10 km (6 miles) of paved road in the whole country; now there are thousands, including 1,100 km (680 miles) of highway from Muscat to Salalah. Amid all this change, traditional ways of life have been remarkably preserved, and the country is more united than at any time in its history.

# A BRIEF HISTORY

### Early times
Around 8000 BC, the area is inhabited by primitive hunters. Agriculture develops on the coastal plain and in sheltered valleys, sustained by the falaj system of irrigation, in around 2000 BC.

### 2nd century BC
Oman is already a trading and maritime centre for boats sailing to India, East Africa and even China. The frankincense trade brings wealth to the Dhofar region.

### 7th–14th centuries
The Omanis are converted to Islam before the death of the Prophet Mohammed in 632. The Ibadhi sect takes the predominant role in the 8th century and imams are elected as religious and national rulers. By the 14th century Sohar is a major port, rich and cosmopolitan through its imports from the East.

### 16th century
In 1507 a Portuguese fleet commanded by Alfonso de Albuquerque arrives off the coast, capturing Muscat, Sohar and other ports, to protect their sea routes to India and the Spice Islands of Indonesia.

### 17th century
Civil war between rival leaders ends when Nasir bin Murshid is elected imam. He unites the country between 1624 and 1649 and starts evicting the Portuguese from their coastal strongholds. Sultan bin Saif succeeds his cousin in 1650. The Portuguese are finally driven out, irrigation systems are repaired, agriculture extended and the navy reinforced until it even chases the Portuguese to India.

### 18th century
Oman takes Zanzibar, off the east coast of Africa, in 1730. Civil war caused by internal rivalry ends with the election of Ahmad bin Said as imam in 1744. In 1783 the roles of imam and sultan are divided between his two sons. Britain is concerned about possible French intervention in the area, and in 1798 signs the first of a series of agreements with Oman, guaranteeing to protect it against aggressors.

## 19th century

Under Sultan Said bin Sultan, known as Said the Great, who rules from 1806 to 1856, the Omani empire thrives. Said adds Dhofar to his realm and controls part of the East African coast, together with ports in Persia and Baluchistan. Upon his death, one of his sons becomes Sultan of Zanzibar, another the Sultan of Muscat and Oman. Britain persuades the new sultan to end trade in slaves and arms, resulting in a great drop in revenues. Led by the imam, the interior rises up against the sultan's rule. Oman becomes a British protectorate in 1891.

## 20th century–present

On the death of Sultan Faisal bin Turki in 1913, the tribes of the interior refuse to accept his son Taimur bin Faisal as ruler. They attack Muscat but are repelled, with British assistance. An uneasy peace is reached between the sultan and the imam in 1920 with the Treaty of Seeb.

Sultan Said bin Taimur succeeds his father in 1938 and embarks on a policy of total isolation from the rest of the world. In the 1950s he moves to take over most of the interior. Revolts are suppressed and peace is achieved, again with British help, in 1959. A long-running border dispute with Saudi Arabia over the ownership of the Buraimi Oasis is settled. Rebellion erupts again in 1963 in the southern province of Dhofar.

Oil is discovered in central Oman and exports begin in 1967 though the revenues are not put to good public use. In 1970, Sultan Qaboos bin Said deposes his father and moves rapidly to improve education, health care, communications and living standards. The Dhofar war finally ends in 1975. Oil output diminishes but prospecting continues, along with steady agricultural and industrial expansion, and a limited development of tourism.

Huber/Schmid

**The country's coat of arms on the gates of the sultan's palace (Al Alam) in Muscat.**

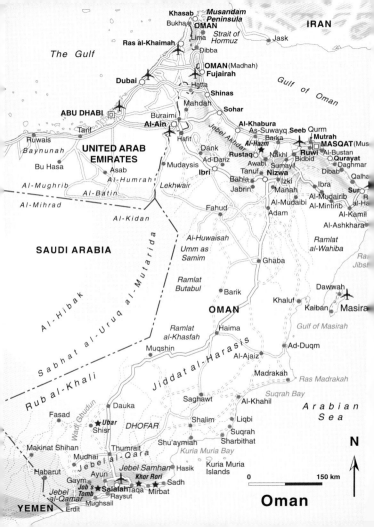

# Sightseeing

### The Capital Area

Greater Muscat is made up of three distinct cities, separated geographically by hills and ridges. Each one has its own particular identity. Muscat is the old port area; Mutrah, to the northwest, is the principal trading district with the country's most important harbour; whereas Ruwi, built on a grid-plan in a valley a few kilometres inland, developed only in the late 20th century into a modern commercial and administrative centre. Still newer appendages to the capital are the largely residential suburb of Qurm, which has two large, modern shopping malls, and Medinat Qaboos with many government buildings, west of Mutrah on the coast. Al-Bustani, south of Muscat, boasts a luxury hotel, a yacht club and leisure centre.

### Muscat

For centuries, visiting seamen have painted or cut the names of their ships on the cliffs which tumble to the sea at Muscat. The word *masquat* means "place of falling", and refers to these precipitous rocks. Nor was Nelson himself too proud to add his own contribution when he came here as a young midshipman. These same rough black hills have allowed Oman's chief city to keep one of its claims to fame: that of being the smallest capital in the world—or so the Omanis say. At one time you could get here only by sea, but today a coast road links Muscat and Mutrah.

Muscat has been the capital since the sultans of the Al-Bu Said dynasty chose it as their residence towards the end of the 18th century. It's a walled town with four gates, which are used nowadays as a practical means of regulating the traffic. The main gate, Bab al-Kabir, serves incoming vehicles, which leave the city by Bab al-Waljat. Bab al-Mathaib is reserved for heavy traffic and Bab al-Saghir for pedestrians and donkeys. Although there is little in the way of "tourist attractions" in the old city, most people love to wander around its steep, narrow streets soaking up the traditional atmosphere. To the right of the British bank, look out for **Beit al-Zubair**, a fascinating museum displaying a collection of Omani jewellery and women's traditional costumes from different regions of Oman.

Walk through the main gate to Wadi al-Kabir. Further on is an old graveyard and further still, you come to **Tawiyan al-Alwiyat**, Place of Wells. One of them is still worked by bullocks.

The city is guarded east and west by two great stone forts,

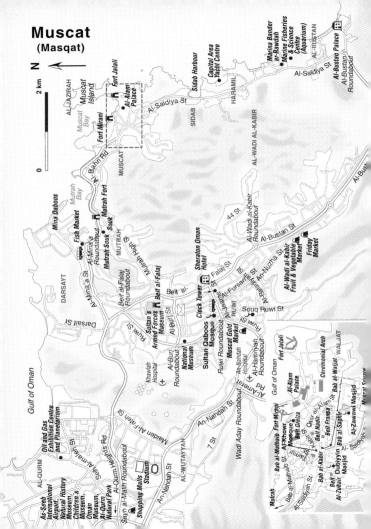

# Muscat
## (Masqat)

N

2 km

0

**Gulf of Oman**

AL-QURM

As-Seeb
International
Airport, Natural History
Museum, Children's
Museum,
Oman
Museum,
Al-Qurm
Natural Park

Oil and Gas
Exhibition Centre
and Planetarium

Sayh al-Malih Roundabout

Al-Qurm Heights Rd

Al-Maha St

Shopping Malls

Stadium

Maidan Ah-Falah St

Al-Nahdah St

AL-WUTAYYAH

7 St

Wadi Aday Roundabout

An-Nahdah St

Al-Amrat Rd

DARSAYT

Darsait St

Mina Qaboos

Fish Market

Al-Mina'a St

Al-Mina'a Roundabout

Mutrah Souk

Mutrah Fort

MUTRAH

Mutrah Bay

Mutrah High St

Ruwi St

Beit al-Falaj Roundabout

Beit al-Falaj

Beit al-

Sultan's
Armed Forces
Museum

Al-Burj St

Al-Burj
Roundabout

National
Museum

Khawlah Hospital

Sultan Qaboos
Mosque

Muscat Gold
Market

Clock Tower

Ruwi Roundabout

Ruwi St

RUWI

An-Nahdah St

An-Nahdah
Hospital

Al-Hamriyah
Roundabout

(Falaj) St

Al-Fursan St

Al-Jaame St

An-Nuzha St

An-Nuzha St

Souq Ruwi St

Sheraton Oman
Hotel

44 St

Al-Wadi al-Kabir
Roundabout

Al-Bustan St

AL-WADI AL-KABIR

Al-Wadi al-Kabir
Fruit & Vegetable
Market

Friday
Market

Al-Bustan St

Al-Bust

Bahri Rd

AL-JAZIRAH

Muscat
Island

Fort Jalali

Al-Alam
Palace

Fort Mirani

Muscat Bay

MUSCAT

Al-Saidiya St

Sidab Harbour

SIDAB

HARAMIL

Capital Area
Yacht Centre

Al-Saidiya St

Marina Bander
ar-Rawdah

Marine Fisheries
& Science
Centre
(Aquarium)

AL-BUSTAN

Al-Bustan Palace

Al-Bustan
Roundabout

**Gulf of Oman**

Mutrah

Bab al-Mathaib St

Bab al-Mahall St

Bab al-Matha'ib St

Al-Saidiyah St

Fort Mirani

Al-Khowr

Al-Alam
Mosque

Beit Greiza

Beit Nadir

Qasr al-Alam St

Bab al-Waljat

Beit Fransa

Fort Jalali

Ceremonial Arch

Al-Zawawi Masjid

Bab al-Sahil

WALJAT

Beit
al-Zubair

Dubiyyin
Masjid

Bab al-Kabir

Beit al-Baraza

Mineral Square

Al-Sadiyah St

built on Arab foundations by the Portuguese in the late 16th century, making the port almost impregnable. Until the 1970s, cannons were fired from the two towers every night as the town gates were dragged shut. Both forts are used by the police and army nowadays, and the public is not permitted to enter, though there is nothing to stop you taking photographs. **Fort Jalali**, to the east, used to serve as a prison. The Sultan's Royal Guard is installed in **Fort Mirani**, where there are still some old bronze cannons.

The Sultan's imposing **palace** stands on the waterfront. You will see fine Omani houses in a combination of Arab, Indian and Portuguese styles, with beautifully carved doors and high walls at least a metre thick, to keep out the heat. Here and there, pink or purple bougainvillaea makes a brilliant splash of colour against the blinding white walls. One of the most attractive of these houses is **Beit Fransa** (once the French embassy and now converted into a museum) near the main gate. **Beit Nadir**, built in the 18th century, is also a museum; it is situated on the main road.

## Mutrah

Although it's also surrounded by hills, Mutrah has more room for expansion than Muscat. Recent development is apparent along the curving seaside road (called the "Corniche"), where modern banks and offices alternate with old Omani and Indian-style houses.

Ships dock at the modern port of **Mina Qaboos**, busy with a mixture of passenger and cargo vessels and time-worn wooden dhows.

**Mutrah Fort**, built entirely by the Portuguese in the 1580s, sits stolidly on a hilltop dominating the bay. Here again, you cannot enter but photography is allowed.

The main attraction for visitors is the old **Mutrah Souk**, full of rich fabrics from India, antiques and pottery, with heaps of colourful fruit and spices. Some of the most popular shops with foreign and local visitors alike are those specializing in silver jewellery. Enter the souk by the main gateway on the coast road, take the first alleyway to the right and you'll find the silver traders beyond some fabric shops.

Mutrah is proud of its new fishery complex, but the old **fish market** on the dhow harbour is still going strong. The market opens at 6.30 a.m.; early morning is the best time to visit. Shell merchants also set up stalls here.

You can take a **boat tour** of the harbours and bays for the view of Muscat which greeted every visitor until recent times—from the sea. Some excursion boats can

# HOLDING THE FORT

Oman's history is written in the stone and mud-brick of its defensive architecture, from the great bastions that guard the coast to the chains of watch-towers that stand like broken teeth on almost every hilltop. Most evocative of all are the historic cities of the interior, former strongholds and palaces of imams and sultans at the edge of the desert. Many are now being restored, using traditional materials and techniques.

Because the two most prominent, the twin sentinels of Jalali and Mirani protecting Muscat Bay, were built by the Portuguese, many others have wrongly been attributed to them. In fact, only a few coastal forts are of Portuguese origin: the vast majority are the work of the Omani Ya'ariba dynasty which expelled the invaders in the 17th century, and the Al-Bu Said dynasty. Many stand on much older foundations; some

dating from the 7th-century Sassanian empire ruled from Persia.

Omani forts are guarded by massive carved wooden portals, with a small cut-out door that admits only one stooping visitor at a time. A slot over the gateway allowed attackers to be drenched with boiling oil or something even nastier, a sticky, superheated brew made from dates! Inside, ceilings are usually of palm trunks supporting palm ribs and mats. State rooms have ceilings of candlewood, often painted with floral and geometric designs. North-facing windows let in cooling breezes while hot air escapes through small openings higher up. A fort invariably has a mosque, separate men's and men's living quarters, soldiers' rooms, prisons, stables for horses, food stores and water cisterns.

**Mutrah Fort looks as though it has grown out of the hill top.**

Pankaj Shah

take you on trips along the coast for swimming, snorkelling and other water sports, landing at one of the idyllic beaches and even providing a picnic or barbecue lunch.

## Ruwi

Many of the essential services that couldn't be squeezed into Mutrah or Muscat are located in Ruwi, and the streets are thronged with an extraordinary medley of nationalities. Ruwi's hotels have become convenient meeting-places for business people, and several little restaurants have sprung up to cater for this transient, cosmopolitan population.

The whitewashed fort **Beit al-Falaj**, north of the town centre, was built in the late 18th century as a summer residence for the sultan. Set amid steep mountain slopes, it controlled the access to the valleys leading to Muscat. In a famous action in 1915, a handful of defenders held out against a force of thousands of rebellious tribesmen. Serving as the armed forces' headquarters until 1978, it has been transformed into the **Sultan's Armed Forces Museum**, run by the Omani army. With its fine carved doors and painted ceilings, the fortress-palace is an impressive setting for displays that trace Oman's history from pre-Islamic times to the recent past, including the defeat of the Jebel Akhdar and Dhofar insurrections. You'll be shown around by a guide.

There is a **souk** in Ruwi but it is modern and cannot compare with that of Mutrah. Ruwi clock tower is a landmark, especially at night when one side of it lights up as a "video-wall" of television screens.

## Al-Bustan

A gently curving bay rimmed by a beach of golden sand, 6 km (4 miles) south of Muscat, or 9 km (6 miles) from Ruwi, was chosen as the site for the first meeting of the Gulf Cooperation Council (GCC) to be held in Oman in 1985. To host the Gulf nations' rulers and their entourages, a spectacular palace and convention centre was built in arabesque style. After the conference, it was turned to good use as a luxury hotel, the **Al-Bustan Palace**. Even if you are not staying there, it's worth a visit; it may be possible to take a tour of some of the halls and rooms.

## Qurm

West along the coast, 6 km (4 miles) from Mutrah, Qurm is a former fishing village which has come up in the world, providing a modern residential area for Greater Muscat. Among the government ministries in the **Medinat Qaboos** quarter on the western edge of Qurm, three museums are well worth visiting if you want to learn more about Oman.

Exhibits in the **Oman Museum** (National Museum) cover the history, architecture and culture of the country, and there's also a display of local arts and crafts. Admission is free, and there's a free guidebook in English. The museum is housed in a small white building next to the Ministry of Information.

Near the Foreign Ministry, the **Children's Museum** has hands-on scientific displays that will interest grown-ups, too. Oman's geography, geology, flora and fauna can be examined in the **Natural History Museum**. The displays describe the efforts being made to protect Oman's wildlife, so beautifully adapted to the often harsh conditions but threatened by loss of habitat and human activities. A new attraction, since the discovery of a whale skeleton, is the Whale Hall.

Two of the capital area's big international hotels are located near the sea west of Qurm, close to a long stretch of superb white sand beach and the yacht club. Between them, there's a small nature reserve where you can spot seabirds and waders, some of Oman's 500 species of birds.

**Camel races** are held on the old airstrip at **Seeb**. The camels, usually so aloof, actually look as though they are enjoying themselves, loping along with strange, rhythmic strides towards the finishing line. The practise of using young children as jockeys has been prohibited; they have been replaced by robots, remotely controlled from cars following them round the track.

## Northern Oman

A convenient day trip west of the capital takes in coastal and mountain scenery, varied villages and a handful of historic sites.

The fort at **Barka**, on the coast 32 km (20 miles) west of Muscat has been restored to an almost too pristine state—it can surely never have looked this clean and perfect in all its history. An inscription records the name of Ahmad bin Said, 18th-century founder of the present Al-Bu Said dynasty and victor in Oman's last, decisive struggle to repel the Persians. Half-hidden among the palm trees behind Barka fort, **Beit Naman** is a fine example of a 17th-century fortified palace.

Inland at the foot of the mountains, warm springs bubble out of the ground at **Nakhl**. Its dramatically sited fortress perches on a precipice, following the contours of the rock so closely that it appears to grow from it. Restoration in recent years may have given it the look of a film set, but in fact the materials used are all authentic—the outside rendering is made from mud taken from local palm groves. From Nakhl's ramparts, on a clear day, you can just see Barka fort on the coast 40 km (25 miles) away.

Near the town of Awabi is the entrance to **Wadi Bani Kharus** which heads into the hills, winding past small villages which cling precariously to its rocky sides. A rugged four-wheel-drive vehicle is essential for this (as for most wadi explorations), and it's a long and sometimes hair-raising drive to the end, but you are rewarded by superb views. Along the way, **Sital** is a picture-book village. An expert local guide will be able to show you ancient drawings on the rocks, depicting animal and hunting scenes.

**Rustaq** served as the capital of Oman at various times during the Middle Ages and up to the early

hemis.fr/Frances

**Back to the wild**. The Arabian oryx, a handsome antelope with long, back-swept horns, a snow-white coat, brown undersides and legs, and black facial markings, is the largest of the region's wild animals. Able to survive the harshest conditions, living on buds, leaves and grass, it once roamed over most of Arabia, and was capable of outpacing its only enemy, man. Then came the all-terrain vehicle and the automatic rifle. By the 1970s the oryx had been hunted to near extinction.

Fortunately, for once, conservationists were a step ahead of the hunters. A few captured animals and a handful donated by zoos became the nucleus of a herd kept in parks in the United States. They soon multiplied, and it became possible to bring about 20 individuals back to Oman. Living at first in pens, they bred well, and several dozen were released into the desert, to be watched over by Bedouin of the Harasi tribe. The process has not been easy. Many of the animals have succumbed to disease or, unable to adapt to the wild after a sheltered life in captivity, starved to death. But today hopes remain high that in the long run the graceful oryx will again be safely established as a living symbol of its desert homeland.

The stunning Nizwa mosque stands in the town centre.

18th century. Its fort, **Qalat al-Kesra**, built over a natural spring, took many epochs to construct, starting with the Persian Sassanid Empire in the 7th century. The main structure dates from the Portuguese occupation, with later additions and extensive modern restoration. Climb up to the turrets for a wonderful view over the surrounding countryside. There is a small souk just outside the fort's entrance, at its most animated on Friday mornings.

Just off the road from Rustaq to the coast, only the brooding bulk of its fort suggests that the village of **Al-Hazm** was once an important centre. Although part of it dates from 1512, according to an inscription on an inner wall, most of the fortress was erected around 1710, the time of Sultan bin Saif II, fifth ruler of the Ya'ariba dynasty, who established his capital here. The depths of Al-Hazm guard his tomb and prayer cell, dark dungeons and, it's said, secret tunnels by which he could come and go. He is referred to in the carved inscription on the main right-hand door; that on the left-hand door bears the date 1162 AH (of the Hegira): around AD 1750.

One of the rooms upstairs constituted a mosque, as you'll gather from the *mihrab*, or prayer niche, cut into the wall, and there's also a Koranic school. In the room directly above the main entrance, note the holes through which visitors were examined, and through which hot oil was poured if they turned out to be unwelcome guests. On the roof you'll see ancient cannon brought from Fort Mirani in Muscat, marked with the royal arms of Portugal. Water from an old *falaj* flows right into the fort, and also irrigates the gardens around it.

## Nizwa

About 170 km (105 miles) from Muscat, the oasis town of Nizwa is a popular destination for day trips and—much better if you have the time—overnight stays. Not only picturesque, it is also the centre of the Omani craft industry. On Friday mornings, people pour in from all over the region to buy and sell livestock and produce at the open-air market. At other times, you'll probably see merchants selling wares from the backs of lorries in front of the blue-domed mosque. But go behind the mosque to find the covered **souk**, largely rebuilt in recent years but still fascinating. If you venture into the back streets you're likely to come across *khanjar*-makers at work.

The 17th-century **fort**, on the other side of the mosque, served for 300 years as palace, prison and seat of government. Its great, round, golden tower, the biggest in Oman, was built in the reign of Sultan bin Saif. It was designed for the new era of the cannon, with gunports commanding a 360-degree field of fire. As

recently as the 1950s, it was the headquarters of the imam, at that time in revolt against the sultan.

## Bahla

An oasis and huge fortress enclosed by a mud-brick wall 12 km (7 miles) long, and reputed as the dwelling place of magicians, witches and soothsayers, this neighbour of Nizwa was the capital city in the 15th century. Oman's diligent restoration teams face a daunting task here; the sprawling, dilapidated ruins, designated a World Heritage Site by UNESCO, tower over 50 m (165 ft) above the surrounding plain. They dwarf today's town, known for its potters who turn out jars and kitchenware, fired in traditional clay ovens—you are welcome to visit their workshops. The central square of the modern town is a lively market, part of it highly specialized, for Bahla is a centre of the date trade.

The fort at **Jabrin**, standing in the middle of the plain near Bahla and 50 km (30 miles) west of Nizwa, was built in the second half of the 17th century as a fortress-palace. One of the finest examples of traditional Omani architecture, it still guards the tomb of its builder, Bil Arab bin Sultan, who died in 1692. Inside, the flowing designs of its painted ceilings, such as the one in the hall of the Sun and Moon, echo

### Dealing in Dates

The centre of Bahla at market time is crowded and the atmosphere reminiscent of the trading floor of a commodity exchange in one of the world's financial capitals. Dealers shout and gesticulate, bargains are struck, promises of future delivery made with a minimum of paperwork. The difference, apart from the open-air setting under a blazing sun, is in the commodity, for here it is dates. Sacks of them lie about, from which samples are constantly being taken and sniffed, squeezed and tasted. Hopeful merchants hold out handfuls for the buyers to try. Clearly there is a lot of expertise involved: anyone who thinks a date is just a date should pay a visit to Bahla.

hemis.fr/Guiziou

# DRESSING IN STYLE

Most Omani men wear a *dishdasha*, a long white gown of cotton or nowadays perhaps a synthetic fabric. Rank can only be guessed from the quality of the cloth and the accessories, a belt with a curved *khanjar*, a turban or cap *(kumma)* and, in cooler weather, a cloak or jacket. A man's turban is formed either from an embroidered Kashmir square loosely wound, or of crisp white pleated cotton cleverly folded so that it keeps its shape even when taken off. But it is the silver-embellished *khanjar* that catches the eye. Worn with pride, the finest examples are treasures of intricate filigree work, with delicate chasing on the blades.

Women are seen in public far less than the menfolk. A stranger arriving in a village might glimpse no more than the end of a gown vanishing round a corner to suggest that the population is not exclusively male, or young, for children are much in evidence. Women traditionally wear a voluminous outer dress or *abaya* over a tunic and trousers. Some, especially in rural areas, cover their nose and mouth—sometimes the whole face—with a black mask or veil. Dhofari women's dress is more colourful, using velvets and bright silks, often gorgeously embroidered. Village children are the most vividly dressed of all, decked out in brilliant fabrics, with gaudy caps, anklets and bracelets and coloured cosmetics in their hair and around their eyes.

hemis.fr/Heeb

the patterns of Persian carpets. The intricately carved wooden balconies and plaster grilles add to the air of elegance.

Jabrin was extensively restored in the 1980s and furnished with various household items to illustrate the traditional life of the region. In case of a siege, its cisterns held plenty of water, and its deep cellars could store a year's supply of dates—practically a complete food, according to the guardians. "Dates and water, that's all they needed to live on!"

**Tanuf**, reached from the road between Bahla and Nizwa, was the scene of tribal warfare in the 1950s. All is quiet these days; you'll find an attractive village and an elaborate *falaj* system. Also set in a wadi in the mountains north of Bahla, the village of **Al-Hamra** with its houses of clay is worth a diversion.

You can hardly distinguish the village of **Misfa** from the cliff face from which it is hewn. Shaded by lemon trees, little streets wind upwards to the different levels of houses, like caves carved out of the rock, with spiral staircases leading to dizzying terraces. Children's faces peer inquisitively from upper windows, only to vanish when you look up at them.

## Sohar

On the coast north of Muscat, Sohar has come down in the world. Once the biggest town on the coast, it now occupies only a fraction of the area it covered a thousand years ago. The legendary home of Sindbad the Sailor, hero of Arab folk tales, it was, according to the 10th-century geographer al-Istakhri, "the greatest seaport of Islam and the most populous and wealthy town in Oman". The Portuguese took it early in the 16th century and made it one of their strongholds guarding the sea routes to India. Above the town rise the six towers of its fort, dazzling white against the blue sea and sky.

Prehistoric remains show that copper was mined in the area in ancient times, perhaps as early as 3000 BC. Narrow tunnels have been found, bored through the rock to the richest deposits of ore, and old spoil heaps and slag from smelting operations dot the hillsides. Mining seems to have stopped around AD 900: it has recently been resumed after a gap of over a thousand years.

## Buraimi Oasis

Inland, across the mountains from Sohar, the large, well-watered Buraimi oasis is divided between Oman and the United Arab Emirates. You can travel to it by road, but you need a visa from the Immigration Department of the Ministry of the Interior. Once through the checkpoint, you can cross between the Omani side and the sprawling modern city of Al-Ain in the UAE. Until the 1950s, the border in this area was ill-defined. An attempt by Saudi Arabia to seize the oasis was thwarted by Sheikh Zayed (later the ruler of Abu Dhabi and UAE President) and the British-officered Trucial Oman Scouts.

Buraimi was a key trading post and crossroads of caravan routes for over a thousand years, and its souks and livestock markets remain a magnet for the Bedouin of the region. Several of the picturesque old forts built to defend it still stand, in contrast to air-conditioned offices and luxury hotels. The battlements of the restored 18th-century **Al-Khandaq fort** make a great vantage point for looking out over the oasis and the desert beyond.

## Musandam

Cut off from the rest of Oman by UAE territory, a mountainous peninsula and a handful of islands form the southern side of the Strait of Hormuz, facing the Iranian shore only about 50 km (30 miles) away. A procession of

Christine Osborne Pictures

hemis.fr/Barbier

The Musandam peninsula is famed for its stunning scenery. | Big earthenware pots from Nizwa with traditional scratched designs make good larders.

Some 3000 *aflaj* irrigation systems still function in Oman.

hemis.fr/Frances

# PRECIOUS WATERS

No one can travel very far in Oman without noticing the beautifully designed stone channels which snake across the land, carrying water from distant springs and wells to villages and irrigating their gardens, palm groves and orchards. For thousands of years—perhaps since 2500 BC— life in this region of no rivers has depended on this complex system, known as *falaj* (plural *aflaj*). To this day, no more efficient method has been found for supplying rural areas; over 70 per cent of Oman's water is distributed this way—a total of 900 million cubic metres of water per year—and 55 per cent of crops depend on a *falaj*.

Construction demands both ingenuity and experience, as well as back-breaking effort. The water must flow down a gentle, steady gradient, so channels can be found carved high up on the steep sides of wadis, passing over aqueducts or through tunnels and even siphons. Friction and leakage are reduced by plastering them with a smooth waterproof cement. Some systems, centuries old, divide the supply from one source into more than 300 channels.

The tapping of underground supplies is especially complicated and dangerous. Their discovery used to depend on water diviners, who could detect a source as deep as 50 m (over 160 ft). A tunnel is excavated by digging vertical shafts every 25 m (80 ft) or so and linking them up.

On the surface, spoil heaps at the top of each shaft show the line followed. The small wiry men of the Awamir tribe are expert at this work; heat and lack of air restricts them to 20 minutes at a time in the narrowest passages.

Surface channels are usually roofed over as far as the edge of a village, to prevent pollution (and to ensure that bans on watering animals and washing are observed). Ownership of the falaj is divided into many shares, determined by the rate of flow and the time of day—traditionally read from a sundial, and nowadays from a clock, at the distribution point. The first water is drawn off for drinking and cooking; below that point there are washing areas for men and women. After washing of clothes and pots, the water enters the irrigation channels of the share-owner's garden.

super tankers passes into the Arabian Gulf, and out again, carrying a significant share of the world's oil. They stick to the Oman side of the strait, watched over by the sultan's navy.

## South of Muscat

The road swings inland and then back to the sea at the old town of **Qurayat**, with its fort, of course, and an endless sandy beach. Four-wheel-drive vehicles can take you on bone-rattling excursions along rocky tracks through the Eastern Hajar mountains and down into wadis lush and green with palm groves and orchards.

To reach Sur, further along the coast, the main road from Muscat makes a long loop south of the Eastern Hajar, skirting the **Wahiba Sands**, a great tract of sharp-edged *barkhan* dunes. Despite initial appearances, this is no lifeless desert; the fragile environment supports a remarkable range of plant and animal life, and has been the subject of a detailed study by scientists. The Bedouin tribes who live on the edge of the sands graze hundreds of their camels and thousands of goats on fresh green growth that springs up if it has recently rained, and on unpalatable-looking thorny scrub if it hasn't.

If you are lucky, you may spot a rare, shy gazelle picking its way daintily among the dunes, or hardly seeming to touch the ground as it bounds towards the horizon.

## Sur

With its natural harbour and perfect location, Sur was a major port for centuries: Marco Polo called in during his voyage in the 13th century and reported that it was much frequented by merchant ships from India, bringing in spices and other goods ad carrying away fine war horses.

It's hardly so busy today, but the beaches are wonderful. **Snisla Fort** with its decorated "wedding-cake" tower has been restored. At the **dhow-builders' yard** just out of town, you'll see traditional wooden craft under construction, using methods that have scarcely changed in centuries. Drills are still driven by a bow and string, and the shipwrights search in their stocks of timber for natural joints, which are stronger than man-made. One concession to modernity: the dhows are fitted with motors and most of them have been stripped of their sails.

Quite close to here, a free ferry crosses the creek to **Ayga**, a small village where the dhow-builders live. It too has a superb fort.

Leaving the harbour loaded with ice, Sur's fishing dhows spend up to two weeks at sea before returning. Part of the catch is dried and used for cattle fodder.

You can take a short excursion by dhow to **Ras al-Hadd**, the headland east of Sur. It is known for the turtles which swim offshore and make their way up the beach to lay their eggs.

Next to the sea northwest of Sur, the ruins of **Qalhat** support Marco Polo's account of its wealth and magnificence. It fell into a decline in late medieval times and was afterwards abandoned, but you can still see the outline of its streets, part of the city walls and the brick tower of the Bibi Maryam tomb.

## Dhofar

Some 1,000 km (620 miles) to the southwest of Muscat on the Arabian Sea, palm-shaded **Salalah** is the provincial capital of Dhofar

**Frankincense.** If you want to take someone a kingly gift, buy some frankincense. In ancient times it was considered to be one of the highest tributes one could offer, as the Magi did to the infant Jesus. Frankincense was thought to have medicinal properties, and was used in embalming—pieces were found in the tomb of Tutankhamun—but most was burned in religious rites; it was believed that prayers were carried to heaven by its scented fumes.

There are only three places in the world where the tall bushes of *Boswellia carterii* or *Boswellia sacra* that produce it will grow: Yemen, northern Somalia and the Dhofar region of southern Oman. The aromatic gum flows from incisions cut in the tree trunks; it hardens into dark amber- or golden-coloured lumps which burn easily thanks to their high oil content.

During the Roman era, it is said that over 3,000 tonnes of it were exported annually from Arabia, carried north by ship and camel caravan for distribution to the cities of the Empire. When Rome declined, Christians and Muslims continued to use incense in their ceremonies, but in far smaller quantities. Exports fell to a few tonnes per year and finally, a modern synthetic substitute developed in Rome destroyed the trade altogether. But local women still scent their hair by wafting it in the smoke, and this gave a modern *parfumier* the idea of creating a new fragrance based on frankincense as well as many floral extracts. You'll find it on sale in Oman, and around the world, in bottles shaped like the handle of a *khanjar* dagger.

Jonas Ramelet

The ancestors of many people living in Dhofar originally came from Zanzibar, a former Omani territory.

Bernard Joliat

**Religious Principles.** Omanis are predominantly Ibadhi Muslim (55 per cent), with Sunni (30 per cent) and Shia (10 per cent) minorities, and some Hindus. The Ibadhi are regarded as more conservative than the other communities, something reflected in their mosques, which are stark and plain. This is one of the earliest forms of Islam, founded less than 50 years after the death of Muhammad, and there are several doctrinal differences with the other schools.

and the second city of Oman. Regular flights link the two centres, as well as comfortable long-distance buses making the 13-hour journey on the smooth, well-engineered highway.

Once a significant port trading in the frankincense extracted from the trees that have grown for centuries on the neighbouring hills, Salalah is now a modern town which has managed to keep much of its charm and character. Small white bougainvillaea-covered houses rub shoulders with office towers; souks and department stores teem with visitors, and the newest and oldest mosques stand side by side. The coast offers superb beaches sheltered by cliffs, with pure white sand lapped by clear, warm seas and soft winds whispering in the nearby coconut and banana plantations. Thanks to the summer monsoon, it is relatively cool and green all through the summer when the rest of the country is baking.

The **museum**, in the Cultural Centre on Ar-Robat Road, contains stones inscribed in ancient South Arabian script, and displays of pottery, tools, weapons, costumes and jewellery.

Some of the objects on show in the museum have been excavated from the **Al-Balid** quarter of Salalah, dating from the 11th century. Excavations there have revealed the remains of a once-magnificent 13th-century mosque, whose roof of carved beams was supported by 136 columns.

The new souk is nothing to rave about, just an ordinary food market, but you may like to visit the **gold souk** on Al-Nahdah Street, to see the glittering selection of oriental and modern gold and silver jewellery.

Along the coast, **Khor Rori**, 40 km (25 miles) east of Salalah, was once the ancient trading port of Sumhuram. This was where the precious frankincense was loaded on ships for export to the east, or on seagoing rafts which took it to Qana in Yemen and from there onwards to Damascus, Egypt and Jerusalem. According

Huber/Bernhart

istockphoto.com/jJeffries

to tradition, King Solomon himself sailed into the harbour, which long since has silted up. Ruins, dating mainly from the 1st century, are currently undergoing excavation.

In the nearby coastal village of **Taqa**, traditional rafts and boats are still made and used in the same way as in ancient times. The house of the *wali* (local chief) is strikingly fortified. Quarries at Taqa provide much of the stone used to face Salalah's handsomer buildings.

About 20 km (12 miles) away at **Mirbat**, many of the houses are built in traditional Omani style, with elaborate carved doors; there's also the inevitable fort and a shark market near the port.

**Mughsail**, 30 km (18 miles) west of Salalah, boasts long, beautiful beaches. They are sheltered by rocky headlands pierced by caves and blowholes through which the sea spouts in rough weather.

### Inland

The Qara mountains *(Jebel al-Qara)* are the home of the mountain tribes, with their large herds of camels and cattle. Here and

**The source of frankincense, *Boswellia sacra*. | Many of the village houses have beautiful hand-carved and studded front doors.**

there a cluster of palm trees betrays the presence of a little village; on rocky outcrops ruined watchtowers point like arthritic fingers to the sky. Families cultivate their land with an ox-drawn plough; the stone channels of an ancient *falaj* bring water from a central well to irrigate fields of onions and garlic, date palms and orchards of cherry and citrus trees.

---

**Weights and Measures**. Today's traders operate in a system as comprehensible as anywhere in the world, and in a straightforward currency, the stable Omani *rial*. But until 1970, the complexities were notorious. Many kinds of money circulated: those of all Oman's neighbours as well as pounds sterling, Indian rupees, US dollars and especially the Maria Theresia *thaler*. The values and weights of various multiples and fractions of these relics (5, 6, 12, 20, 24, 120) made up competing but overlapping regional systems. Few outsiders and not all locals ever understood them, so there was general relief when simplification was decreed as one of the earliest moves towards modernization. One exception survives: silver is weighed in *tolas* (deriving from *thaler*). One *tola* = 11.75g.

Excursions into the Jebel al-Qara and its wadis by four-wheel-drive vehicle include the natural springs of **Ain Arzat**, the well-watered Wadi Darbat, and the pools of **Ayun**. It's worth a diversion to see the mysterious prehistoric standing stones in **Wadi Ghudun**. Generally grouped in threes, they may mark ancient burial sites. **Wadi Hanun** was once a collecting point for the frankincense where it was stored before being carried north by camel caravan or south to the ancient port of Sumhuram.

The area around **Thumrait**, 80 km (50 miles) inland, is noted for its wonderful desert scenery. To the north stretches the long black line of the asphalt highway to Muscat, following an ancient caravan route through the Jiddat. Harsh as this landscape may seem, it is home to the Harasi, a Bedouin tribe that probably originated in Ethiopia and speak their own language. Old watering holes are marked by a few crumbling buildings sinking slowly into oblivion, replaced by their modern equivalent—rest houses and petrol stations.

Near the little oasis of Shisr, north of Thumrait, the ruins of **Ubar** lay hidden beneath the sand until the 1990s. Archaeologists have excavated some of the remains, which are perhaps not particularly spectacular, but are of

A typical living room or *majlis*, where objects are kept in large coffers and the seating is the floor.

istockphoto.com / McIntosh

great historical interest. The town, once on the frankincense route, is estimated to be 4000 to 5000 years old, and knew a great period of prosperity thanks to its strategically favourable location.

Still further inland, straddling the border with Saudi Arabia, is the fabled **Rub al-Khali** ("The Empty Quarter"), a moonscape of sand dunes, sparse thorn bushes and rocks where only the hardiest Bedouin or the best-prepared expeditions can travel.

# Dining Out

Many visitors choose to dine in hotels where the menus are international but with the bonus of fresh locally caught fish and seafood—the prawns and spiny lobsters can be excellent. An Indian curry or two and some Arabic specialities add a touch of exotica. Alcoholic drinks are available in the larger and more expensive hotels: elsewhere the choice is restricted to water and soft drinks, sometimes fruit juice.

The big towns have good Chinese and Lebanese restaurants, sometimes in upmarket versions. To eat economically, head for an Indian restaurant, where the food will be tasty if not always varied. The Muscat area has the same fast-food outlets as any other capital city, most of these establishments being centred in Ruwi.

Because of all the outside influences, dishes with a genuine local flavour are few and far between. They are based mainly on lamb, sometimes elaborately prepared, subtly spiced and almost always accompanied by rice. A whole roast lamb is the centrepiece of most feasts; on lesser occasions there are kebabs: chunks of lamb or meatballs grilled on a skewer.

For dessert there may be fruit; *halwa*, a thick paste made from nuts, honey, butter and spices; or the inevitable dates—to an Omani, especially someone from the interior, no meal is complete without them.

## Hospitality and Courtesy

Should you be invited to an Omani home, you will be expected to remove your shoes and sit on a rug on the floor. Take care that when you sit the soles of your feet do not point towards anyone: it would be considered an insulting gesture in most Arab countries. Use only your right hand to eat, drink and pass things.

Tea or coffee is usually offered, and you would be discourteous to refuse it. The coffee is excellent and often spiced with cardamom. If you don't want any more, cover the cup with your right hand. It's polite to accept a second cup, but you should not drink more than three.

You'll find a wide choice of silver jewellery in the Nizwa souk.

# Shopping

Silver jewellery is probably the best buy in Oman. Traditional designs are intricately worked, and range from delightful little kohl boxes to ornamental chest pieces, sometimes with bronze, gold, coloured glass or old coins worked in. You're not likely to find anything more than 50 years old, as traditionally most jewellery was part of a bride's dowry, and was melted down after its owner's death. Jewellers also sell the handsome silver Maria Theresia dollar *(thaler)* coins, first minted in late 18th-century Imperial Austria. Despite the date 1780 which appears on them, most were produced much later, from the 19th century right up to modern times—silversmiths from Beirut to Dubai are still making perfect copies, with the right silver content of about 20 grams.

A symbol of virility, the beautiful curved *khanjar* daggers, with finely worked sheaths, scabbards and belts, were made traditionally with handles of rhinoceros horn. Though shopkeepers may try to convince you they are selling you the real thing, the handles nowadays are generally made from plastic or wood. In any case it is forbidden to import rhino horn into most countries. If you do buy a dagger, don't pack it in your hand luggage.

Brass and copper objects make attractive souvenirs, particularly the coffee pots with their curved spouts. You'll also find enticing selections of fabric from many exotic places, especially Kashmir shawls (which many Omani men wear as turbans), highly coloured dress lengths, saris, robes and caftans.

There's a whole range of spices to bring Middle Eastern and Indian flavours to your cooking, and fragrant rose or orange blossom water from the terraced gardens of the Green Mountain.

# PRACTICAL INFORMATION

**Business hours**. The banks are open in principal Saturday to Wednesday, 8 a.m.–12 p.m., Thursday 8 a.m.– 11 a.m. Offices are generally open Saturday to Wednesday, 7.30 a.m.– 2.30 p.m. Shopping centres open Saturday to Wednesday, 8 a.m./ 1 p.m. and 4 p.m.– 8 p.m. and Thursday 8 a.m.– 1 p.m.

**Currency**. The Omani *rial* (OR or OMR), divided into 1,000 *baisa*. Coins from 5 to 50 baisa; notes from 100 baisa to 50 rial.

**Climate**. Generally hot and humid on the coast, cooler in the mountains. Around Muscat, the small amount of rain falls mainly between December and March. In the south, the rainy season is from June to September.

**Clothing**. Lightweight washable cottons are recommended, with something warmer for nights in the desert. Dress modestly, to comply with Muslim traditions. Shorts are frowned upon, whether for men or women. Trousers are acceptable for women, as long as they are loosely cut: avoid anything tight or revealing. Sunglasses and a sun hat are essential.

**Electricity**. 220/240V AC, 50 Hz.

**Health**. Precautions against malaria are advisable if you are visiting Musandam, although the risk is small. Take any medications your are likely to need during your trip.

**Language**. Arabic. English is generally understood in the Muscat area and in business and government circles and is taught in schools.

**Photography**. Ask permission first. Men and children are usually quite happy to be photographed; women will usually refuse, or turn away as soon as they see a camera. You should not take photos of any military sites.

**Safety**. As in all the countries of the Gulf, there is very little crime. You will generally feel safe, even if you wander around on your own. Commonsense precautions should be taken. Women should not wear scanty or revealing clothing to avoid harassment.

**Time**. GMT + 4, all year round.

**Tipping**. Where a service charge has not been added, 10–15% should be added to restaurant bills. Taxi drivers and porters also expect a tip.

**Water**. Tap water is drinkable in the cities and towns. In the villages, stick to bottled drinks.

The Kaaba in Mecca, the holiest of Islam's holy cities.

# SAUDI ARABIA

The kingdom of Saudi Arabia extends over four-fifths of the Arabian peninsula. To the northwest, it is bordered by Jordan, to the north by Iraq and Kuwait, to the east by the Gulf, Qatar, Bahrain, the United Arab Emirates and Oman, to the south by Yemen and to the west by the Red Sea.

The discovery of oil in the 1930s, its large-scale exploitation by the Americans since 1945 and considerable rise in the price of oil in the 1970s have completely transformed the country, forcing it to confront full-on the challenges of modernity full on. With 25% of the world's reserves, it is the number one producer and exporter of oil.

Visitors are bound to be impressed by the quality of the infrastructure, the resolutely modern architecture of the public buildings, the gigantic scale of the shopping malls displaying the whole world's brand names, the number of limousines cruising along the broad straight avenues, as well as the diversity of ethnic groups and cultures co-existing in a land area of 2,253,000 sq km. The country's population of 27.6 million includes near 9 million foreign workers, mostly Asian and Arab.

However, this impression of modernity and cosmopolitanism is inevitably modified by the endurance of customs that come as a surprise even to visitors coming from other Arab or Muslim countries. Think, for example, of the women covered from head to toe in black abaya overgarments gliding silently through the shopping malls, where some shops close five times a day at the hour of prayer, just as civil servants interrupt their work to go and pray in the nearest mosque. On the other hand, as a direct consequence, Saudi Arabia is recognized as a country where people's security and the safety of personal property are unrivalled.

A majority of Saudis are Sunni Muslim, following the Wahhabi doctrine that lays down a strict code of conduct. The Shia make up 5–10% of the population, living mainly in the east and at the border with Yemen.

# A BRIEF HISTORY

**5th–1st centuries BC**
Tribes originating from present-day Iraq settle in the Arabian peninsula. From the 3rd century Arabia forms part of Nabatean kingdom bordering on the north at Damascus, now capital of Syria.

**6th–7th centuries**
The prophet Mohammed is born in Mecca in 570. In the surrounding hills, he is subject to numerous visions and hears the first verses of the Koran. Forced to flee the town in 622, he returns eight years later to dedicate the sacred Kaaba stone cube to Allah, the one God.

**18th–19th centuries**
A kingdom grows out of the alliance between the tribe of the Al-Saud and Mohammed ibn Abd al-Wahhab, a Muslim reformer. The strict form of Islam he advocates, known as Wahhabism, is adopted. The Ottoman Empire conquers Arabia in the 19th century.

**20th century–present**
The kingdom is proclaimed in 1932 by Abd d-Aziz ibn Saud gathering under his rule the regions conquered by the Turks since 1902. The country takes on its present name. The king fathers 45 sons, the oldest of them succeeding him on the throne at his death. Saud reigns from 1953 to 1954 but clashes with his brother Faisal, pro-Western and conservative, who seizes power in 1964. Assassinated in 1975, Faisal is replaced by his half-brother Khalid, followed in 1982 by Fahd Ibn Abd al-Aziz Al-Saud. In 1991, the American-led multinational force deployed on Saudi territory intervenes in the Gulf War against Iraq. King Fahd dies in 2005, and his son Crown Prince Abdullah, de facto ruler from 1996, ascends to the throne. For the first time, in November 2005, two women are elected to the Chamber of Commerce and Industry in Jeddah.

Saudi Arabia originates an Arab peace plan providing for general normalisation of relations with Israel in exchange for withdrawal from all Occupied Territories to pre-1967 borders. Adopted at a summit conference in Beirut in 2002, the plan is re-launched in 2007 at an Arab summit in Riyadh. The kingdom settles frontier disputes with its neighbours on the Cooperative Council of Arab States in the Persian Gulf and with Yemen. In addition, Saudi Arabia carefully cultivates its influence within the Muslim world. Through the Organization of the Islamic Conference, the authorities are eager to present an image of a moderate Islam.

# Sightseeing

### Riyadh

The royal capital and important business centre is a modern city, built at an altitude of 800 m. The name Riyadh (which means "Gardens") first appeared in the 18th century. The Al-Saud family, which had chosen Diriya, a town nearby the present capital, as the headquarters for their campaigns, did not occupy Riyadh until 1773. The success of Wahhabism prompted the intervention of Mehmet Ali who destroyed Diriya and razed the walls of Riyadh in 1824. The city fell into the hands of Ibn Rashed in 1891 and was recaptured in 1902 by the future King Abdul Azis bin Abdul Rahman Al-Saud who thenceforth made it his capital.

**Masmak** fortress is the only remaining trace of the ancient city. Inside is a museum devoted to Ibn Saud.

**Riyadh Museum** presents a very broad panorama of the history of the country and region from the Stone Age through to the Islamic era.

Some 30 km from town, the **camel market**, open for business every day, is one of the largest in the Middle East. Once a year, the king organizes a race in the middle of the desert. More than 2,700 camels (actually, they are dromedaries, with one hump) "trot" at 60 kph over a racetrack 22 km long. There's no betting. The winning jockey receives a gold dagger, a large sum of money and, a sign of the times, a tanker-truck to transport water.

istockphoto.com/jamjoom

## Jeddah

The city, once known as "the Bride of the Red Sea", is said by legend to be the place Eve came to when driven from the Garden to Eden. Jeddah in Arabic means "Grandma", the affectionate nickname by which the people know Adam's companion, believed to be buried in Jeddah.

Located on the coast of the Red Sea, this most pleasant of the country's large cities is regarded as the gateway port and airport for the holy cities of Mecca and Medina. The little fishing port founded in 647 by Caliph Uthman was an obligatory port of call on the Gulf's incense and coffee route. At the beginning of the 19th century, the growth of coffee exports from the West Indies, competing with coffee from Yemen threatened the port of Jeddah. In 1869, after the opening of the Suez Canal, freighters travelling between Arabia and the Mediterranean no longer stopped off at Jeddah, but it profited from an increase in shipping on the Red Sea. In 1947, Ibn Saud decided to modernize the city and razed most of

istockphoto.com/Salem

**One of Jeddah's landmarks, the Floating Mosque on the edge of the Red Sea. | A tapline carries oil from Saudi Arabia through the desert to Lebanon; it was completed in 1950.**

the old town quarters, in particular the city-wall and the five double-doored gates which had closed every evening.

Although it has given way to modernity, Jeddah has nonetheless preserved some of its old residences of the 18th century, built with coral from the Red Sea. They are to be seen when walking through the old quarters. The **Municipal Museum** is housed in a 200-year-old dwelling that is itself to be admired as a fine example of this unusual architecture. The museum exhibits a collection of photos on the evolution of the city.

Other museums, such as the **National Museum** (in King Abdul Aziz Palace), the **Ba Junaid House Museum**, **Tayebat Museum** or the **Abdul Rauf Khalil Museum** with its display of 10,000 objects tracing the history of Jeddah and the Saudi legacy, all serve to enhance the town's standing. Try to find time, too, to visit the **Islamic Academy of Fiqh** or the **Castle of Cultural Arts Museum**, belonging to the renowned Saudi musician Tarek Abdel Hakim, to discover a unique collection devoted to art and to musical instruments.

Among the major sights to visit in this multi-faceted city is **Al Balad**, the historic centre where you can visit **Bayt Nassif**, a magnificent restored dwelling symbolizing Jeddah's rich past and

transformed now into a cultural centre. Built between 1872 and 1881 for Sheikh Omar Effendi Nassif, then Governor of Jeddah, this 106-room edifice was built so that camels carrying goods could climb the stairs leading to the kitchen up on the fourth floor.

The superb **Makkh Gate**, known as Bab Ashlam, is one of the oldest in the country and reveals a

**Mohammed**. Son of Abdullah, Mohammed is a member of the Hashemite clan of the powerful Quraish tribe from Mecca, where he was born around 570. Tradition sets the Prophet's Koranic revelation in his 40th year. In the midst of his meditations in a cave near Mecca, the Archangel Gabriel commanded him to "read" (Koran means "reading") and dictated to him the verses of the Holy Book. The pagan Quraishi disapproved of Mohammed's monotheistic preaching and in 622 (according to the Christian calendar) the Prophet moved to Yathrib, the future Medina— beginning of the Hegira (Hijra), flight and starting point of the Islamic calendar. He returned to Mecca in 632, his head held high, for a first pilgrimage which then became annual. Before he died, Mohammed fixed the rite for the Muslim pilgrimage.

The King Fahd Fountain in Jeddah is one of the tallest in the world, its jet reaching a height of 312 m.

Turkish influence in its construction. It is main entrance for pilgrims making the *hajj*. On the edge of the Red Sea, the **Floating Mosque** (or White Mosque) seems to merge with the water.

But the town has now also become a major modern urban centre, one of the richest in Asia. Avant-garde buildings stand side by side with splendid palaces, in particular along grand thoroughfares like Al-Malek Street (King's Highway) or Sultan Street, while several works of art in various styles stand in the middle of endless boulevards. The seashore in the western part of town has been laid out as a Riviera-style **Corniche** on the model of the Croisette in Cannes or the Promenade des Anglais in Nice. It is one of Jeddah's most elegant tourist sites stretching about 100 km. In the evening, young couples like to stroll along it, admiring the sunset. You may be surprised to find a series of fine sculptures along the way, executed by such great artists as Joan Miró and Henry Moore, one of them a masterpiece that defies the Islamic tradition forbidding the creation of figurative images. In addition, within the framework of a gigantic project of urban development likely to cost several millions of euros financed by private sponsors, the Corniche is to be further beautified by the installation of permanent laser projections and other original artistic creations. Modern architectural projects include the completion in 2010 of the Lamar Towers—with a fantastic panorama promised from the 65th floor.

The city has countless parks and gardens as well as the **King Fahd Fountain**, one of the biggest in the world, spouting water 312 m into the sky. This is a particularly splendid sight at night when it is lit up.

Families will enjoy the fun of various amusement parks such as **Al-Shallal** with its skating rink and impressive helter-skelter, **Atallah Happyland**, **Sannabel** and **Sindibad**.

Jeddah and its environs cater in particular to shopping and sporting activities. Saudis are indeed fanatical about their cricket, bowling and deep-sea diving, this latter pastime attracting visitors from all over the world, thanks to the sea's remarkable and well preserved bio-diversity. Festivities celebrate religious holidays such as Aid-el-Fitr (or Aid-el-Seghir) and Aid-el-Adha (or Aid-el-Kebir), cultural events—Al-Janadriyah and Al-Mizmar—or plain social: Summer Festival in June and July.

Of course, sun, sea and sand here mean fantastic beaches, marinas and water sports facilities at Durrat Al-Arus, Shums, Salhia, Albahar and Al-Remal, all blessed with great coral reefs.

Medical tourism is a little-known aspect of Jeddah. Its clinics are highly reputed and waiting lists are long. Many travellers like to combine their visit here with a stay at clinics famous for their dental care, ophthalmology or plastic surgery. The town numbers more than 40 large hospitals, independently of the abundance of private specialist clinics.

## Mecca

Signs on the motorway on the approach to Mecca indicate different directions for Muslims and non-Muslims: access to the holy town is reserved for Muslims only (the same rule applies to Medina).

The Muslim tradition says that Ibrahim (the Biblical Abraham) led one of his wives, Hajar (Hagar) and his son Ismail (Ishmael) into a valley of Arabia. God caused a spring to gush forth beneath the foot of Ismail to give him water to drink. The caravans passing this way were able to use the spring water that they named Zemzem. Merchants decided to settle in this place and thus the town of Mecca was born. Tradition adds that Ismail, aged 13, and Ibrahim erected the Kaaba as a shrine.

Located in an oasis 73 km from Jeddah, Mecca dates back to classical antiquity and represents a way-station on the ancient caravan routes used by merchants and pre-Islamic fetish-cult pilgrims. Islam's holy of holy cities, Mecca is the destination to which all Muslims are supposed to go at least once in their life and to which they turn to say their prayers.

This pilgrimage or *hajj* is one of the five Pillars of Islam and takes place in the Islamic month of Dhu al-Hijjah. It grants forgiveness for the sins of the pilgrims and its focus is the Kaaba, a cubic stone and marble edifice 15 m high and 12 m wide, the "Sacred House of God" sheltering at its northwest corner the Black Stone, a meteorite offer to Ibrahim (Abraham) by the Archangel Gabriel. It is completely draped in black silk and is now to be found within the precincts of the Great Al-Haram Mosque, which can hold up to 300,000 worshippers.

For the ceremony of the *hajj*, men dress in a simple hemless white robe, wear sandals and no hat on their head, which is entirely or partially shaven. women must cover their hair with a headscarf. After prayers, pilgrims enter the courtyard of the Great Mosque, where they have to circle the Kaaba seven times. A few get to touch the Black Stone, and the luckiest can actually kiss it, always in a reverential manner. The pilgrim then goes on to the Rock of Abraham to pray, then finally walks seven times between Safa and Marwa, two hills near the town, recalling the path that Hagar took in search of water for her son.

## Medina

This is the second holy city of Islam at an altitude of 594 m and 350 km from Mecca in the most fertile part of Hejaz. Driven from Mecca, according to Islamic tradition, by Allah, Mohammed found refuge here and died here June 8, 632. The town, known as Yathrib in pre-Islamic times (Lathrippa in the texts of Ptolemy) took the name of Medina, in Arabic al-Madinah al-Nabi (City of the Prophet) or al-Madinah al-Munawwarah (the Enlightened City). Historians observe that the town has over 100 names. Medina shelters the tomb of Mohammed and his daughter Fatima-Zahra, who also died in 632, as well as those of the first caliphs, Abu-Bakr and Omar Ibn al-Khattab. Although the pilgrimage to Medina is not prescribed by the Islamic creed, many Muslims do go there to pray in the **Prophet's Mosque** (Al-Masjid al-Nabawi), erected on the site of the original mosque.

istockphoto.com/Salem

**The slender minarets of the Prophet's Mosque in Medina.**

# Dining Out

Local cuisine is often highly seasoned and spicy. The staple food item is the flat round unleavened *pita* bread accompanying all dishes. *Mezzeh*, the equivalent of hors d'oeuvre (starters) may number as many 40 dishes. Rice, lentils, chickpeas *(humus)* and cracked dry wheat *(burghul)* are all very common. The most usual meats are mutton and chicken. Goat or camel meat is also quite frequent. Beef is rare, and pork is forbidden by Islamic law.

**A traditional lantern that could well light up your Arabian Nights.**

The main meal of the day is lunch. It consists of *kultra* (meat kebabs) served with soup and vegetables, grilled chicken, rice with spicy lamb, salads, *kabsah* (the national Saudi dish of chicken and rice), *mufallaq* (wheat ground and cooked with chopped onions, spices and tomatoes), *biryani* (a rice dish with mutton steamed in a pie crust).

Arabian pastries, cream desserts and rice pudding *(mahallibiyah)* are commonly on the menu.

In traditional Arab cuisine, dairy products are widely served, as Bedouins are very dependent on their herds for their food. Fish are also popular. *Hutte sijan* (small perch seasoned with garlic, lemon and cumin) and *hammour samak* (a white, thick-fleshed fish akin to grouper) feature among local fish dishes.

All the big towns have international restaurants, above all Chinese and Thai, as well as well-known fast-food chains. Jeddah is distinguished for its fine little fish restaurants all along the Corniche highway.

### Drinks

There are no bars as these are known in Europe or America. Law strictly forbids importing and consuming alcohol and heavy fines are imposed if the law is breached. Arab coffee and fruit juices are very popular alternatives. Non-alcoholic beers and cocktails are served in hotel bars.

## Shopping

Apart from Bedouin gold and silver jewellery and embroidered fabrics, you will not find a large range of local craftwork. The bazaars of Al-Alawi, Khamis Mushayt and Najran in Jeddah are among the most interesting in the country, but you must really hunt around to find original prayer-mats or antique knives and swords. On the other hand, you'll have no trouble finding a great range of shoes, incense and spices.

The Al-Balad quarter is one of the main tourist attractions, a veritable shopper's heaven mixing the most famous and fashionable brand names on Tahlia Street and traditional bazaars on Gabel Street.

# PRACTICAL INFORMATION

**Business Hours**. Banks are open Saturday to Wednesday 8 a.m.–noon and 5–8 p.m. Shops generally open 8 a.m.–10 p.m. Museums close Friday. All public places and shops close during the hours of prayer.

**Climate**. Temperatures are generally scorching and often reach 45°C or more, especially between mid-April and October. But they can go down to around 15°C in December and January, and even lower at night in the desert. On the coasts, it's hot all year round, dry in winter and humid in the summer.

**Clothing**. Women should take great care about how they dress. The recommended garment is some form of the *abaya*, a long black dress covering the whole body. Men should always wear long trousers, avoiding any kind of shorts or bermudas.

**Electricity**. You will come across both European 220 V and American 110 V, so be sure to have an adaptor with universal plugs.

**Health**. Since water is not everywhere drinkable, it is better to drink water in sealed bottles. Avoid ice cubes, fresh fruit juices, raw vegetables and unpeeled fruit, as well as under-cooked fish, meat, poultry or milk. Don't walk barefoot on the sand or damp floors and don't stroke stray animals. Be sure to pack whatever medication you anticipate needing for the journey.

**Internet**. Access to Internet is authorized in Saudi Arabia but subject to censorship. High-speed (ADSL) links are possible, but with limited capacity.

**Language**. The official language is Arabic, but English, the language of business, is widely spoken in the towns.

**Money**. The currency unit is the Saudi *riyal* (SAR) divided into 20 *quirsh* and 100 *halalas*. Cash-distributors (ATM) accept Visa and Mastercard bank-cards. However, traveller's cheques are difficult to exchange. In town, many restaurants and hotels accept payment by credit card.

**Safety**. Westerners should be prudent—without being paranoid—and are advised to consult regularly the security communiqués put out by their embassies. Park cars in supervised areas and check that they are locked.

**Time Zone**. GMT+3 hours, no daylight saving time.

A heart-stopping view over the terraces of the Highlands.

# YEMEN

Yemen lies in that part of the Arabian peninsula the Romans called *Arabia Felix*—"Happy Arabia"—as a tribute to its arable land and the prosperity it enjoyed from exporting frankincense and myrrh to the Ancient World. For most of its history, the country way a collection of kingdoms or sultanates, sometimes warring. From these disparate factions, two modern states emerged in the 1960s: the former Yemen Arab Republic, or North Yemen, and the ex-People's Democratic Republic, or South Yemen.

In 1990 they proclaimed their unification, calling the new state the "Yemen Republic". With Sanaa as its capital, it has a population of 21.8 million people in an area of about 530,000 sq km (205,000 sq miles).

The Yemeni people are almost 100% Muslim—both Sunni and Shia, with small Christian and Hindu communities and a Jewish minority. Families are large, with the roles of men and women strictly defined. The men take care of public duties, while the women are responsible for the home and family.

The most important source of revenue is the export of oil and its derivatives. After the country was unified, tourism developed as the second-most significant resource, followed by agriculture and fishing, but the economy only started to improve in the late 1990s.

Yemeni men often wear a kilt (*futa*) or a wide-sleeved robe (*zana*). They cover their heads with a stiff skull-cap, sometimes used as a basis on which to drape their turban. The dagger (*jambiyya*) is both an arm and a symbol of pride. Women in Aden wear either European clothes or the shapeless black *shaider*. In the countryside, their dress is colourful and may take be an embroidered tunic and skirt worn over long trousers caught in at the ankles. Veils are regularly worn.

All told, Yemen is an exciting blend of modern ports and inland towns and villages continuing in their age-old ways.

# A BRIEF HISTORY

**10th–2nd centuries BC**
The Kingdom of Sheba supplies the ancient world with frankincense and myrrh, transported by sea and overland by caravan. According to tradition, Shem, the eldest son of Noah, founded the city of Mahrib. In 115 BC the Himyarite dynasty is in control with its capital at present-day Dhafar.

**4th–7th centuries**
Judaism and Christianity are introduced. Conflicts erupt between the two religions, and in 525 the Christian Ethiopians intervene. Their presence is short-lived and is followed by Persian domination until 628 when the governor is converted to the new religion of Islam. From then, Yemen is ruled as part of Arab-Islamic caliphates. Christianity fades shortly after the introduction of Islam but a Jewish colony lives on in Yemen until the creation of Israel in 1948.

**16th century**
In 1516 the Mamelukes of Egypt annex Yemen, but in the following year the governor surrenders to the Ottomans. The Turks remain until 1630. Afterwards most of the country is ruled by the Zaidi Imams.

**19th century**
The British take Aden in 1839; it is of prime importance for their access to India. They administer the south from Bombay. The opening of the Suez Canal in 1869 makes Aden even more vital. Towards the end of the century the Turks once more occupy large parts of Yemen.

**20th century–present**
After World War I, an imamate, the Kingdom of Yemen, is established in the north. Aden officially becomes a British Crown Colony in 1937. In 1958 the Kingdom of Yemen joins the short-lived United Arab States with Egypt and Syria. The 1960s mark the outbreak of revolution and civil war—in 1962 the north forms the Yemen Arab Republic, or North Yemen; Aden and the south achieve independence in 1967, and in 1970 declare the People's Democratic Republic, a Marxist state. The two Yemens form a united Yemen Republic in May 1990. The world nods approval over Yemen's first multi-party elections in 1993, but the precariousness of the union is revealed in May 1994 when the south attempts briefly to break away but fails. Constitutional amendments are made in 2000 and 2001. The government is fighting rebel groups.

# Sightseeing

The topography of Yemen varies from tropical coastal fishing villages to temperate high plateaus. The scene is endlessly enchanting, whether you are visiting nomadic tribal lands of the north or a modern urban agglomeration with a maze of an old city at its heart.

## Aden

Arriving by sea your first sight is the impressive backdrop of dark volcanic mountains, with Aden nestling at their foot. The largest of these is Mount Shamsan, which rises to a height of 540 m (1,775 ft).

The city itself is divided into several districts, Steamer Point (now called Tawahi) being the passenger port. You may like to look in at the famous **Crescent Hotel**; its elegance fled with the British but you can still sense a certain ghostly colonial grandeur. The country's history comes to life at the **National Museum**, one of the most important in the country. Its treasures include a group of half-life-size alabaster statues unearthed from the excavations of various towns of the Awsan kingdom, a rival of Saba.

Maala is a dock and industrial area, through which you have to pass to reach **Crater**, a district dra-matically bound in on three sides by barren rock. There are still a few old houses worth seeing.

Make a point of visiting the extraordinary **At-Tawila Cisterns** on Mount Shamsan: 18 of them, thought to have been built by the Himyarites in the 1st century. The idea was to catch the water gushing down from the mountaintop. You can still see remains of the special marble paste used to line the tanks. In the surrounding garden stands the **Ethnographical Museum**, where you can admire textiles and daggers.

Find time to visit the **Airdus Mosque** and an edifice known simply as the **Minaret**, thought to be the remains of an 8th-century mosque. The dazzling white tower was restored in the 18th century.

The most interesting fort is on Mount Seera Island, a spot that has become a seaside resort for local people. **Gold Mohur Beach** is marked by a lighthouse at the southern end and a hill fortified with ancient Turkish cannons; Alghadir Beach has a central hill with remains of old fortifications.

## Taizz

One of the roads leading to the north from Aden passes through Taizz, a former capital city. Its location at 1,400 m (4,600 ft) in the foothills of Jabal Sabir, the highest mountain in Taizz Prov-

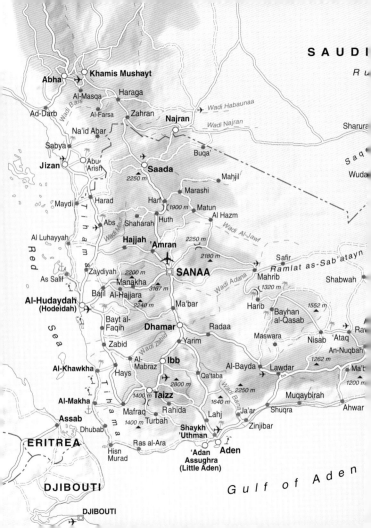

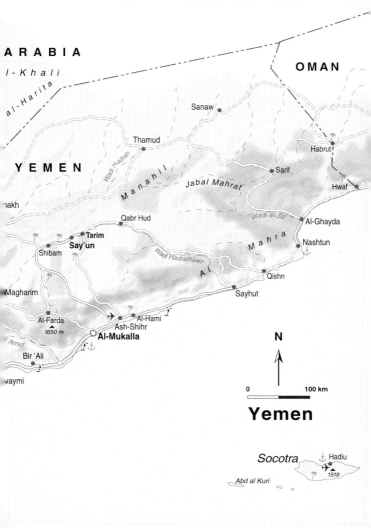

ince, assures it more moderate temperatures than the coastal towns. One highlight is the lively **market** at the foot of the northern wall of the old city, in which unveiled women merchants, noted for their tough bargaining, are to be seen—a rare sight in Yemen on both accounts.

The city is dominated by the **Fortress of Cairo** (Al Qahira) high on its cliff, in military use and therefore out of bounds for tourists. They can, however, enter the former palace of Imam Ahmad, now the **National Museum**. Everything has been left just as it was when the imam died in 1962, supposedly to demonstrate the social iniquity of his rule prior to the revolution in the north. **Salah Palace** also belonged to the imam and is similarly a museum.

## Zabid

Zabid ranks as one of Yemen's oldest towns. The university here dates from the 9th century; its biggest claim to fame is the creation of algebra by one of its scholars. Though much diminished now, from the 13th to the 15th centuries it was the focal point of Sunni teaching for the southern part of the Islamic world, and the town harboured 236 mosques. The points of interest today are its old walled souk, some large houses—sober on the street side, but splendidly ornamented within—and the citadel's palace, now a government building.

## Hodeidah

The city of Hodeidah is the hub of the region known as Tihama, the coastlands of the Red Sea. These hot, sand-blown flatlands with their predominantly black peoples make a contrast to the cooler highlands with their Semitic population. Slavery and long-term migration from East Africa account for the Tihama's racially diverse make-up. As the source of almost half of the country's agricultural production, the Tihama is Yemen's most economically important region.

Hodeidah is a relatively young city. It was only from the middle of the 19th century that the Turks began to turn it into an efficient port in response to the British development of Aden. Progress was set back when the city was bombarded during World War I. In 1934 the Tihama was coveted by Saudi Arabia, but since the skirmishes of that year between the two countries, Hodeidah has been able to develop in tranquillity. At the time of reunification of the two Yemens it ranked as Yemen's second most important port.

A stroll through the oldest part of the city, near the market area, can be rewarding. The typical old Red Sea houses here are three or four storeys high and feature wooden balconies or window covers—Turkish style —and interesting plaster-ornamented walls. You might be surprised to recognize Indian decorations on some of the doorways—they were executed by the craftsmen who used to follow in the wake of sailors and traders to the ports of the Red Sea coast.

If the truth be told, there are few other charms to Hodeidah. Its touristic importance lies more in its convenience as a stopping point en route to more interesting outlying sights. About an hour away to the south by road, for example, **Bayt al-Faqih** attracts visitors from far and wide to its famous Friday market, established in the early 1700s for trading in coffee beans. (The word "mocha" derives from the nearby port of Al-Makha, or Mokka, where rich coffee merchants exported their products in the 17th century.) Apart from coffee, you can buy every sort of fruit and vegetable and handicraft.

hemis.fr/Guiziou

**What's Qat?** The former People's Democratic Republic did its best to quash the qat-chewing habit, but it's still enjoyed throughout Yemen. Qat (pronounced *gat*) is a green leaf with mild euphoriant qualities which grows in the high country. It is customary for almost every Yemeni man to spend the greater part of the afternoon in a social group chewing his way through several bunches of qat shoots, bought fresh each day. The leaves are not swallowed but held in a wad in the side of the cheek and spat out at the end of the session. Cigarette and hookah-smoking are part of the ritual and the chewers refresh themselves frequently with sips of water, lightly flavoured with cinnamon or clove—although cola-based drinks are catching on. Women chew less than men: they say it spoils the shape of the face.

It is maintained that the leaf is not addictive. It can have harmful physical effects, but the real damage is economic. All activity stops for the daily ritual, large sums are spent, families suffer and coffee plantations are torn up and replaced by this more remunerative crop.

## Sanaa

Once you have seen the capital, altitude 2,350 m (7,750 ft) and known as the "pearl of Arabia", you'll understand why UNESCO saw fit in 1984 to take the magical city under its protection. The ensemble of mud-brick ochre "skyscrapers", trimmed in elaborate white alabaster and plaster-work and fitted with multi-coloured windowpanes, is one of the most beautiful sights in the world.

Yemeni folklore relates that Sanaa was founded by Noah's son Shem. It's also said that during the period of the Sabaean and Himyarite kingdoms in Yemen, Sanaa had a great palace 20 storeys high, as well as a splendid cathedral that drew Christian pilgrims from all over Arabia. Nothing remains of either of these edifices, today, but the memories are still kept alive.

With the advent of Islam, Sanaa's fortunes alternated between prosperity, when it was the capital either of a region or of all of Yemen, and destruction, as sultans seized power from each other. The last conquerors were

**The method of building multi-storey houses of dried mud bricks has not changed in two thousand years. The ground floor sheltered animals and is now used mostly for storage.**

the Turks, who held the city for a second time from 1872 to 1912. The civil war in the north in the 1960s began in Sanaa. After it ended, the city began to expand outside its walls and the population exploded as well. Today it is a bustling city with an estimated population of 1.8 million, complete with traffic jams.

Within the modern exterior, Sanaa has one of the largest completely preserved walled cities, or **medina**, in the Arab world. Its eastern part, at the very least, begs to be explored. Here are found the most imposing of the fabulous tower houses. Photogenic subjects present themselves everywhere as you wander among the beautiful houses, mosques and souks. Note, too, the many *hammams*, or bathhouses, dating from the Turkish era. You may be lucky enough to catch a glimpse of some of the private gardens adjoining the houses and mosques, pleasant oases in the urban maze. The western part of the medina is less exotic, as it consists largely of newer buildings. But even there a few beautiful old houses remain among them, as well as the old embassies and the former Jewish quarter.

**Bab al-Yaman**, or Gate of Yemen, is the break in the old city wall at the southwest part of the medina. The square here is full of animation at almost any time of day. The largest city market in Yemen, *Suq al-Milh*, begins at the gate and extends half a kilometre north within the medina. It is grouped into some 40 areas, each specializing in a particular kind of merchandise. Outside of the medina, to the east, lies the **Suq al-Qat**, a market devoted primarily to the green leaf beloved of most Yemeni men.

The Suq al-Milh snakes its way past the **Great Mosque**, built around AD 630, when the Prophet Mohammed was still alive. It is certainly worth inquiring whether you may enter to see its richly decorated interior. Some of Sanaa's other **mosques** can be appreciated from the exterior, such as the Al-'Aqil Mosque, whose beautiful minaret rises over Suq al-Milh. You can also step back to get a good view of Qubbat al-Bakiliya, on Al-Liqiya Street in the easternmost sector of the medina. It dates from the early 1600s, when the Turks first occupied Yemen. Not surprisingly, its numerous cupolas reflect the Turkish style.

The newly renovated **National Museum** will give you a good overview of Yemen's history, covering pre-Islamic ancient kingdoms such as that of Saba, and Islamic times. Exhibits include papyrus fragments, coins, weapons and statues.

Shades of ochre in Shibam, a stunning mud-brick city of tower houses in Wadi Hadhramawt.

## Mahrib

Mahrib is the old capital of the kingdom of Saba. Lying east of Sanaa on the ancient frankincense trade route, it prospered from the taxes levied on passing caravans. The Great Dam Mahrib constructed in the 8th century BC to irrigate fields of cereals and palm oases was a stunning feat of engineering in its day. It was washed away in AD 570. Head for the archaeological sites to see the remains of Sabaean temples and the ruins of the sluice gates of the ancient dam. The old village on a hill apart from the new town is made up of mud skyscrapers, mostly abandoned. Integrated into the foundations of the houses are stones from ancient monuments, bearing inscriptions and designs.

## Manakha

Some 90 km (56 miles) west of Sanaa, on the road to Hodeidah (the first modern thoroughfare built in the country), the village is the main economic centre of the region. It stands on a height at 2,200 m (7,218 ft) in the midst of the cultivated terraces on the slopes of Jebel Haraz. In recent years it has been expanded and modernized, but the old streets of the centre have retained their charm. Do not miss the Sunday market, where local produce is sold.

Manakha is an ideal base for visits to neighbouring villages.

## Al-Mukalla

Capital of Yemen's largest province, in the eastern part of the country, Al-Mukalla is a wealthy seaport and fishing centre on the Gulf of Aden. Its white waterfront houses, with their engraved wooden window blinds and balconies and turquoise decorations, make a pretty sight. When you walk around the old town, note the handsome **Rawdha Mosque**, one of the finest of Mukalla's many beautiful places of worship.

The **Al-Mukalla Museum**, near the bay, is housed in what was once the palace of the sultans. The building has been renovated to display the folklore and antiquities of the region.

If you visit Al-Mukalla, do not fail to venture north into the **Wadi Hadhramawt**, one of Yemen's major attractions. The biggest river valley in the Arabian Peninsula, the wadi runs for 160 km (95 miles), fertile and green on its banks, through stone-strewn desert plateaus. It is located on the ancient incense route—frankincense was in fact grown on its banks—and was prosperous in those bygone centuries, when its waters were used in intricate irrigation systems.

It was here in the wadi that Yemen's tower-house style of

Huber/Gräfenhain

**Sartorial Splendour.** What does the well-dressed Yemeni male wear? In the West, a gentleman puts on a tie to appear at his best; here at the edge of the Arabian Peninsula he slings a Kalashnikov over his shoulder. The dagger worn at the waist has been a requisite Yemeni masculine ornament for eons, but nowadays the average man has a wide choice of weaponry: souks are stocked with old hunting guns, automatic rifles, bazookas and hand grenades. It's mostly show — all that steel is reserved for harmlessly shooting off a few rounds with a flourish on special occasions like weddings or Friday outings, and, of course, for self-defence.

building originated. In the dry season, brick-making can be seen everywhere. At **Shibam** you encounter the tower houses of mud bricks at their most exquisite: the southern counterpoint to Sanaa. Here are assembled some 500 beautiful "skyscrapers" of as many as 13 storeys, giving rise to the epithet "Manhattan of the desert". As it did for Sanaa, UNESCO has undertaken a programme of preservation. The best thing to do here is to wander around the town's narrow streets along with the goats, and to photograph the town at sunset from the cliffs above the suburb of Sihayl.

Further into the wadi lies **Say'un**, largest town in the valley. For 500 years, until the 1967 revolution, a North Yemeni tribe made it their capital, building some of the most beautiful mosques in all of Yemen. Dominating the "town of a million palm trees" is the stunning white-plastered Sultan's Palace. The archaeological and folklore museum installed within fills only a small part of the immense structure. The Tomb of Habshi also cries out for attention with its turquoise splendour, but it dates only from the 1910s.

**Tarim** has been an important centre of Islamic teaching for centuries, and it boasts some 365 mosques. The square minaret of the most famous among them,

Al-Muhdar, is 50 m (164 ft) high and is depicted on virtually every brochure describing the wadi. The town is distinctive for its displaced architecture—South-East Asian baroque! It seems that many Yemenis returning home from places such as Java and Singapore—numbering 300,000 in the 1930s—were rich enough to build huge palaces.

## Dining Out

Traditional Yemeni cooking is done in a *tannur* or pottery oven set in sun-baked bricks. Cereals are the basic foodstuff, served with vegetables, or meat. In the south a lot of fish and rice is eaten. Tourist hotels serve European food.

Normally a meal begins with radishes and onions, followed by sweet dishes flavoured with honey and butter. Then come savoury dishes using mutton or beef if they are available. The national speciality is *helba*, a kind of thin stew which is eaten using flat *khobz* bread to scoop it up.

The traditional way for a family to eat is with the right hand from a communal bowl. In larger gatherings there are separate receptacles for men and women.

Tea may be served, but the favourite drink is *qishr*, coffee made from the husks and flavoured with ginger, cinnamon

hemis.fr/Guiziou

**Country women in the Hadhramawt region wear straw hats with high pointed crowns.**

or cloves. It was first choice in the harems of Turkey and is often known as "sultan's coffee". It is poured into small cups without handles (you hold them delicately from underneath on the tips of your fingers) and is the usual beverage offered to visitors.

## Shopping

The silver markets in the souks of Sanaa, Taizz and Hodeidah are a popular hunting ground for tourists, but be aware that the

Huber/Gräfenhain

Mark Ellis

objects may contain relatively little silver and have often been treated to look old. Gold jewellery may be of good value, as supposedly it is sold strictly by the gram, with no value added for the craftsmanship. *Do* have an idea of gold prices in advance. The curved tribesman's dagger worn by men on a belt, known as the *jambiyya*, makes a good purchase. The model worn by the elite classes, the *dhuma*, is richly ornamented with silver and gold. A water pipe *(madaa)* will require plenty of space to carry home, as it typically stands a metre (3 ft) high, and a bulky tripod stand goes along with it.

Other ideas include pottery, in particular the tiny cups for serving *qishr*, jars, urns and vases of all sizes. There are plenty of brilliantly hued hand-woven and dyed fabrics available. Some of the Yemeni embroidery is superb. Look out, too, for the fragrant spices, perfumes and small boxes of incense, but don't forget the little earthenware stand needed for burning it. Of interest to philatelists are the first-day covers available at post offices.

So many *jambiyya*, which one to choose? | Yemeni honey is considered a precious gift, and is said to cure diseases. The most famed variety is called Al Elb.

# PRACTICAL INFORMATION

**Antiques**. It is against Yemeni law to export anything over 40 yers old without official permission.

**Business Hours**. Banks open from 7.30, 8 or 9 a.m. –noon or 12.30 p.m., depending on region. Closed Friday. Post offices open Saturday to Thursday 8 or 9 a.m.–noon or 1 p.m. In the north, they open also 4–8 p.m.

**Courtesy**. Visitors will want to respect the customs of the country by not wearing shorts, sleeveless shirts or short skirts. Do not take photographs of people without asking their permission. Women should avoid gazing directly into the eyes of local men; even smiles can be misinterpreted.

**Climate**. There are several distinct climatic regions in the country. The southern and Red Sea coasts (including Aden, Al-Mukalla and Hodeidah) lie in an arid, hot zone. Sanaa, in the central highlands, enjoys milder temperatures (maximum 25–30°C year-round, minimum 0°C January and 10°C July), with rainy seasons in March/April and August, when travelling is difficult. A general rule is to wear loose, cool clothing, hat and sunglasses.

**Credit Cards**. Generally accepted only in large hotels, and even then not all types are recognized. There are not many cash dispensers (ATMs).

**Currency**. The *riyal*. Coins range from 1 to 20 *riyal*; banknotes from 50 to 1000 *riyals*. The easiest currency to change is the US dollar. Travellers cheques in US dollars or sterling are advised.

**Health**. Malaria risk exists throughout the country except in Sanaa.

**Holidays**. May 1 and 22, Sept. 26, Oct. 14, and Nov. 30. If a holiday falls on a Wednesday or a Sunday, most stores will be closed for a long weekend (from Wednesday to Friday or Friday to Sunday).

**Language**. Arabic. English is generally understood in large towns.

**Taxis**. It is advised to negotiate the price of your ride *in advance*.

**Telephone**. IDD is available in some parts of the country. Mobile phone coverage is good in the west and the coastal areas of the east. There are Internet cafés in the towns throughout Yemen.

**Tipping**. Virtually unknown. Service is included in restaurant and hotel charges.

**Water**. Drink bottled water, and bring along salt tablets. Avoid swimming and paddling in fresh water.

Reading from right to left: beautiful Arabic
calligraphy.

# LOCAL CUSTOMS

This tourist destination clearly appeals to people searching for a different place to go whether by air or on a cruise ship, but before visiting the Gulf States (which do not include the Republic of Yemen) it is important to know something of local customs.

## Islam

The Gulf Arabs are Muslims who believe in the revelations of God as made to their Prophet Mohammed and recorded in the holy book or Quran (Koran).

The five pillars of Islam have remained unchanged since the early 7th century. They consist of: the *shahadah*, the pronouncement that "There is no god but Allah, and Mohammed is his messenger"; *salat*, prayer at the five prescribed times each day; *zakat*, giving alms; *sawm*, fasting during the month of Ramadan; and *hajj*, performing the pilgrimage to and associated rites at Mecca at least once in a lifetime.

Certain religious taboos affect visitors to the Gulf. Paramount is the prohibition of alcohol by the more conservative states of Saudi Arabia, Kuwait and Sharjah in the UAE. Alcohol cannot be imported into Saudi Arabia and Kuwait, and anyone caught in its possession risks severe penalties, which may include flogging.

Muslim dietary laws also forbid the sale or consumption of pork.

During the month of Ramadan, the dates of which vary from year to year, everyone, regardless of their faith, is required to observe the fast in public. This means no eating, drinking or even smoking between sunrise and sunset. If caught doing so, besides angering the local people, in some countries you could end up in prison.

The Gulf States make it plain they do not care for non-believers to enter their places of worship. But if ever you do have the opportunity to enter one, cover your head and remove your footwear before going inside. As a measure of respect, avoid approaching a mosque during prayers.

Friday is the Muslim holy day, when offices and most private businesses are closed.

## Minding Your Manners

Etiquette is taken very seriously at all levels of society in the Gulf

States. When a person enters a room, it is usual for everyone, women included, to stand up and shake hands. A foreign man, however, should wait for an Arab woman to offer her hand to him first. Foreign women may be rebuffed if they offer their hand to an older Arab, or to one who has just performed ablutions prior to prayer.

Like all Muslims, people use their left hand to cleanse themselves and only the right to help themselves to food. Accept refreshments and use your right hand if you find yourselves in a traditional setting. Discard your shoes at the door of a house and, when seated, ensure the soles of your feet are not displayed.

Apart from in Saudi Arabia, where it is a general term of respect, the title "sheikh" (feminine *sheikha*) in the Gulf applies only to members of the ruling families. The rulers of Kuwait and Qatar carry the more formal title of Emir. The only sultan is the ruler of Oman, and until Bahrain became a kingdom in 2002, the only king was the custodian of the holy places in Saudi Arabia.

Do not take photographs of people without their permission. Armed with this small amount of knowledge, you will be able to mingle in local society with confidence.

## Tips for Women

Although the number of Arab women participating in the local workforce is increasing, a woman's role in traditional Gulf society remains little changed. Progress has been made, and women now make up half the students at GCC universities, but it is necessarily slow, because Islamic law still conditions women to accept a restricted lifestyle.

Many women continue to wear the veil whenever they venture outside the family home, and entertainment is often supervised by a brother or male cousin. The occasional Arab woman drives a car—except in Saudi Arabia where women drivers are banned—but a woman shopping in the souk without friends or older adult females is rare. Because independence as defined in the West is not well understood, it is sensible for women visitors to observe a few rules.

Choose your wardrobe carefully for a visit to any of the Arab States. Pack loose-fitting cotton trousers or mid-length skirts. Shorts, T-shirts and bikinis are acceptable around the hotel pool, but dressing like this in the street or on the beach will invite comment.

Bahrain and Dubai are more relaxed, but the Gulf States in general remain very conservative. Any woman who does not wear an *abaya* or robe or cover her hair risks arrest by the mattawa or religious police in Saudi Arabia. If you are correctly attired, there is nothing to prevent you going out to the shops alone, but it is prudent to return to your hotel before nightfall. A group of women might safely take a taxi to the beach, but it is not advisable to do so alone.

Crime against women is very rare in the Gulf, but do not leave yourself exposed. Avoid eye contact with Arab men in your hotel; women on business should not accept to meet someone without first checking them out. Always tell the doorman where you are going and ask him to call a taxi rather than doing so yourself.

## Tips for Businessmen

The modern Arab merchant is likely to be well travelled—many are educated abroad—and to have a keen understanding of Western business methods, as well as being able to conduct discussions in English. Even if his manner appears casual, do not underestimate his shrewdness.

**Henna designs bring blessings, as well as good luck, joy and beauty. | Coffee forms an essential part of everyday sociability. | Many women cover themselves completely outside their homes.**

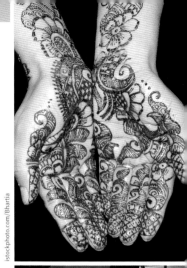

istockphoto.com/Bhartia

Bernard Joliat

Christine Osborne Pictures

Take your time over an appointment in the Gulf, where traditional courtesies are valued. Impatience is likely to be fatal, because most Arabs feel they have all the time in the world.

Be punctual for an appointment. It is polite to enquire about your host's family, but not specifically his wife. Accept the ceremonial *gahwah* or local coffee—you will cause offence if you don't. If you are the host, you should be the one to offer refreshments. When you have finished your cup, hold it up in your right hand and rock it back and forth gently to indicate you want more. If you have had enough, cover your cup with your hand.

If you are marketing a product, a low-key presentation, perhaps a video or computer-animated graphics, is a good way to begin, but talk only to the decision-maker.

A good sign is an invitation to dinner in a hotel restaurant or at his family home. And while Friday may be imminent, do not try to conclude arrangements. Stay on and accept a trip out on his boat or driving in the dunes. Doing business is second nature to an Arab and liking you is as important as liking what you want to sell him.

If you conclude a deal, on the next occasion take your wife, if you are married. Your host's wife will love entertaining her for coffee and henna mornings and visiting the souks. The Gulf States are ideal for combining business and a holiday.

## Gulf Cooking

Up to the 1970s, local cooking was limited to basic Bedouin food—dates and fish, or mutton eaten with rice and unleavened bread. Today, the Gulf boasts restaurants from all over the world, along with traditional Middle Eastern cuisine comprising specialities such as the array of appetizers known as *mezze* and stuffed lamb or *khouzi*.

Seafood is a favourite main course. Most menus feature grouper *(hammour)*, fried or baked with *tahini*, ground sesame seed sauce. Stuffed fish *(samak mashi)*, tuna steaks, grilled sea bream and prawns are also popular. A local variety of lobster known as *umm robien* is a familiar item in seafood banquets.

Many visitors enjoy a trip to one of the colourful Gulf fish markets.

Chicken dishes range from American-style takeaway and other fast-food outlets, which the Arabs adore, to elaborate poultry recipes served in up-market hotel restaurants. Meat is generally imported beef or lamb which is eaten with home-grown vegetables and salads.

Along with traditional dates, the Gulf States now grow citrus fruits and strawberries, as well as pineapples, papaws and bananas, in the semitropical southwest corner of Saudi Arabia and Dhofar.

## Beverages

Saudi Arabia, Kuwait, Qatar (except in special bars and restaurants of the international hotels) and Sharjah prohibit the sale and consumption of alcohol. Elsewhere, alcohol is available in hotel bars and restaurants. There is a huge choice of soft drinks and fruit juices, while excellent local mineral water is sold throughout the region. It is advisable to stick to bottled water as tap water is not drinkable everywhere.

## Health

Strict health and hygiene standards are maintained throughout the Gulf, with regular inspections made of places preparing food. A result is that visitors are rarely ill with the "upset tummy" common in many hot countries.

There are no special health requirements for visitors, although anti-malarial precautions are advisable in southern Oman. For outdoors, you will need a sun block of a high protective factor, at least 25. Avoid catching a cold after coming in from the heat. A warm jacket or wrap around your shoulders is a good idea in many chilly, super air-conditioned hotel restaurants.

## Money Matters

Each Gulf State has its own currency, the Omani *riyal*, in Bahrain and Kuwait a local *dinar*, the UAE *dirham* and so on (for details see the Practical Information pages for each country). In most States there are no restrictions on the import and export of monies, and local currencies are freely convertible. Visitors arriving by air may feel more comfortable obtaining some currency at the airport, but the best value is via local exchange dealers in town, who also keep more convenient hours than banks.

Many major banks are based in the Gulf State capitals, and the well-known credit cards, such as Visa, MasterCard and American Express, are widely accepted. Sterling or dollars are usually the best for cash transactions, and traders will expect you to bargain.

Tipping is not encouraged or expected, but migrant workers performing menial tasks appreciate any gratuities.

Most Gulf States charge a departure tax. All the airports have banking, telecommunications facilities and duty-free shopping for cigarettes, alcohol, watches and gold jewellery, as well as raffles for the latest car models—it could be your lucky day.

**General Editor**
Barbara Ender

**Editorial Assistant**
Petronella Greenhalgh

**Design**
Karin Palazzolo

**Layout**
Luc Malherbe
Matias Jolliet

**Maps**
JPM Publications

**Photo credits**
p. 1 Bernard Joliat
p. 2 istockphoto.com/Banks
(falcon); /Bhartia (hands);
/Johnson (mosque).
Neil Perrinjaquet (portrait)

Copyright © 2009, 1997
JPM Publications S.A.
12, avenue William-Fraisse,
1006 Lausanne, Switzerland
information@jpmguides.com
http://www.jpmguides.com/

Printed in Switzerland
12614.004523
Weber Benteli/Bienne
Edition 2009